lower

IGNITING

SPIRITUAL

AWAKENING

THROUGH

RADICAL

HUMILITY

lower

zach
meerkreebs

New York • Nashville

FaithWords
Hachette Book Group
1290 Avenue of the Americas, New York, NY 10104
faithwords.com
@FaithWords / @FaithWordsBooks

First Edition: January 2025

FaithWords is a division of Hachette Book Group, Inc. The FaithWords name and logo are registered trademarks of Hachette Book Group, Inc.

The publisher is not responsible for websites (or their content) that are not owned by the publisher.

The Hachette Speakers Bureau provides a wide range of authors for speaking events. To find out more, go to hachettespeakersbureau.com or email HachetteSpeakers@hbgusa.com.

FaithWords books may be purchased in bulk for business, educational, or promotional use. For information, please contact your local bookseller or the Hachette Book Group Special Markets Department at special.markets@hbgusa.com.

Print book interior design by Bart Dawson.

Library of Congress Cataloging-in-Publication Data

Names: Meerkreebs, Zach, author.
Title: Lower : igniting spiritual awakening through radical humility / Zach Meerkreebs.
Description: First edition. | New York : Faith Words, 2025.
Identifiers: LCCN 2024031692 | ISBN 9781546007517 (hardcover) | ISBN 9781546007531 (ebook)
Subjects: LCSH: Revivals—Kentucky. | Asbury University. | Religious awakening—Christianity. | Humility—Religious aspects—Christianity.
Classification: LCC BV3774.K4 M33 2025 | DDC 269/.2409769—dc23/eng/20240903
LC record available at https://lccn.loc.gov/2024031692

ISBNs: 9781546007517 (hardcover), 9781546007531 (ebook)

Printed in the United States of America

LSC-C

Printing 1, 2024

To my sweet Kristin Joy…

and all of the other hidden and humble heroes

who have changed my life.

contents

Foreword

"We should go to Asbury," my friend Freddy said as we were visiting Nashville. I was tired and didn't feel the need to go, despite the buzz about a revival, an awakening, or an outpouring happening there. (No one knew what to call it!) I was speaking at a conference and had a podcast recording nearby. Freddy, one of our church's worship leaders, was also leading worship at the conference. Did I mention I was tired? I took a nap in our hotel room and woke up fifteen minutes later with a clear prompting from the Holy Spirit: "Go to Asbury."

I asked Freddy, "Are you ready?"

Without hesitation, he shouted, "Let's go!"

We started the four-hour trek and arrived after dark. The campus of Asbury University was crowded, so we parked on a lawn, then walked to a line of people wrapped around the chapel. When we finally made it in, I headed to the balcony. It was standing room only. The aisles and every square inch of the room were filled with people. On the stage, a group of students led worship in a stripped-down, basic, humble, meek, and unassuming kind of way. It wasn't "excellent" in a polished, professional sense.

With skepticism in my heart, I found a spot up high and noticed an old projector in the corner, seemingly untouched since 1992. I took a picture of it with my phone. Then I opened my Bible and started reading in the midst of the singing. I didn't know what to expect, but I wanted to encounter God. And encounter Him, I did.

As the crowd took over singing "Agnus Dei," the Holy Spirit moved powerfully. "Holy...Holy...Are You Lord God Almighty...Worthy is the Lamb...Worthy is the Lamb...For You are HOLY..." I can still hear it. I stood up, swayed, and sang at the top of my lungs. Time stood still. It felt like only twenty minutes, but hours passed by.

I eventually met Zach Meerkreebs, the preacher whose message sparked all of this. He was a little stripped down, basic, humble, meek, and unassuming. With a round face, curly hair, glasses, and a soft smile, he exuded kindness and a deep love for Jesus. He wasn't surprised by what God was doing, more grateful. "I just preached a stinker," he told me he had texted his wife after his sermon. But the students stayed. Then their friends came, and soon people from all over the country and the world followed.

I took off my sweater and gave it to Zach, sensing he'd be there for a while. He thought I was as weird as I thought he was. After all, who says "stinker"?! I found Freddy, and we left. But a part of me stayed in that chapel, and a part of that chapel stays with me.

Since that day, I've gotten to know Zach better. His life is marked by a deep, rare sense of humility. He is a man of prayer who loves to talk about his wife and their daughter in heaven. He's a wounded man whose faith has been tested by fire. It's no surprise that God has used him as He has.

Paired with the Gospel of Jesus Christ, I believe Christ-like humility is the most important message for the United States right now. In fact, the whole world so desperately needs this message. Humility is the *missing* virtue and that has created so much division in our land. What if we started pursuing and reclaiming it?

I pray that I would walk with a greater humility, and I know all who read this book will shed pride with every page turn.

As we seek to go lower, who better to lead us than the man God used to lift us all up once upon a time? After all, Jesus was a little stripped down, basic, humble, meek, and unassuming. Zach will show us how to be more like Him.

Jonathan Pokluda
Pastor, author, and friend

Introduction

An Ordinary & Unremarkable Chapel Service

"Laid a stinker. Be home soon."

"They aren't leaving...maybe I'll still be able to make it home to take a nap."

insert GIF shared only between a post-preaching husband and a gracious wife...

"Babe, something is happening. Please pray."

"KP...I won't be home for dinner. Bring the girls to Asbury asap."

Fast-forward sixteen days, and the world had been shaken by God pouring out His love and meeting tens of thousands with His peaceful power. Sixteen days of unending worship coupled with moments of testimony, the reading of Scripture, preaching, healing, miracles, teaching, and silence. This experience had been in a beautiful and fragile auditorium of a faithful Christian liberal arts university in small-town USA.

Camera pans through rolling green hills, past horses grazing, to Wilmore, Kentucky...traveling up the steps of Hughes Auditorium, the chapel of Asbury University. Go Eagles!

On February 7, 2023, I had been given the gift of facilitating a day of soul care and spiritual formation for youth ministers in Columbus, Ohio. For my dear friend Ciro and me, the day was full of honesty, hunger for a deeper relationship with God, and practices that could possibly serve those in the room. After a day of ministry, marked by sweet teaching moments and soft hearts to receive, I jumped into my car and embarked on my three-hour drive home. I needed to get home, though it would be very late, so that I could complete my two-part sermon out of Romans 12 to preach at Asbury University the next day.

Of course I prayed and listened to sermons during my drive home while simultaneously receiving prophetic visions...

Not.

I listened to a true crime podcast, called a friend, and ate Twizzlers to stay awake.

The next morning, I woke up relatively early and drove to a wonderful coffee shop near Asbury where I created slides based on the preparation I had done. Romans 12:9–21 only includes thirteen verses, but on the topic of loving others, it includes twenty-eight commands that set the bar pretty high.

How will I preach this message?

How can I get this all in in the time allotted?

This was my last of fourteen sermons preached within two and a half weeks, and I was wiped. This is not to impress (small flex), but a public confession that I need to learn the word *no*. I would talk to my counselor again and again about pace in the coming weeks.

When will I get a nap?

As I prayed and prepared for the coming chapel service, I felt God invite me to present a challenge to the students: that they could not love others based on the standards laid out in this passage. Not only did the number of directives I'd need to cover make me nervous, but the idea of preaching *that* kind of sermon to *these* kinds of students when I am not usually *that* kind of chapel speaker made me a bit uneasy.

I wandered up to the balcony, took a picture of the empty auditorium, and posted it on Instagram, asking for prayer for this place and the students who would soon fill those seats. If I'd only known…

The gospel choir arrived. Several of them described the prior night's worship and prayer, testifying to feeling that God was going to move in the chapel that day. If we'd only known.

Their faith and willingness to lean into the service encouraged me, but I'm sad to say I placed their comments in my back pocket instead of letting them sink into my heart. I was tired and a bit nervous for my sermon.

The student chaplain prayed for our service, and the choir began. Benjamin Black, the choir director, led the students through persistent, faith-filled, God-honoring songs. His energy contrasted with the sleepy voices of students in sweatpants, some of them wearing earbuds and scrolling through their phones. Then I came up to preach.

Did I feel the wind at my back or have an open vision of me stepping into the throne room? No...I asked the students to open their Bibles to Romans 12 and began.

"I hope you guys forget me but that anything from the Holy Spirit and God's Word would find fertile ground in your hearts and produce fruit."

Had two cherubim given me high fives on my way up onstage or massaged my shoulders when I thought I'd forgotten my clicker? No. I began reading the Scripture about becoming "Love in Action."

The week before, I'd given a sermon to these same students that I was much more confident in on the cost of pride, competition, and comparison. I'd challenged the students to lean into greater gratitude, understanding that everything we have are gifts, and to gaze upon Jesus...no one else.

But I dove into the verses that were set for February 8: Romans 12:9–21.

"Do you love me?" I asked. I invited them to look at their neighbor, whom they were assigned to sit by, and ask the same question. After hearing some awkward giggles, I spoke about three of my favorite places in my town that I love. A favorite restaurant where my wife and I do date nights, a coffee shop where I sip cappuccinos, and a gelateria my seven-year-old specifically loves. But these places, though remarkable, could not stand up to the people I introduced next whom I have genuine love for: Kristin, my wife; and our daughters, Eden, Esther, and

Mercy. I wanted my love for them to be without hypocrisy… love that was not fake, nor selfish nor violent.

Hypocritical love in this day and age is a point of pain for many, especially those who sit on our college campuses. These students leaned in as I read the verses describing real love and calling out fake and selfish love. Our souls, I explained, are designed to be loved and to love. When that love is a counterfeit, though, it only fills the space temporarily, possibly to meet an immediate need, and quickly disappears like hands full of sand running through our fingers. We are, as Christ followers, invited to be both the object and the agent of God's love, His affection and mission.

This real love is hard for us to just muster up. We cannot white-knuckle godly love. We have to experience it. We need to realize that "we love because he first loved us" (1 John 4:19).

To truly love those around us and expand that love to the ends of the earth, we must experience God's love in an authentic and personal way. As my friend Ciro often says, we will need to sit as the object of His affection and love before being the agent of it. And we must always return to it to continue being a representative of God's love. If all it took was just knowing everything about God's love, the Sadducees would have gotten it. If we only needed to do all the perfect things, or do all the things perfectly, to love God and others, the Pharisees would have had this down. No, we have to experience the love of God for ourselves, truly be saturated in it, before we can spill out that love toward others. This love is what the students and staff at Asbury University would encounter in profound ways for the following sixteen days.

My time was running out, so I clicked through my slides to the last one that had three questions:

 What is the source of your love?
What is the purpose of your love?
Who are you becoming through this expression of love?

When I finished, I invited the students and staff to stay if they wanted to talk and pray or come to the altar to experience God's love firsthand through the Spirit. Then I offered more encouragement before leaving:

"Do not leave here until you experience the love of God so that you can pour it out."

"The world needs these kinds of Christians. People that have experienced the love of God."

"I pray that this sits on you like an itchy sweater... that you have to itch. That you would need to do something about it."

"Jesus, do a new thing in our midst. *Revive us by your love.*"

I sat down in the creaky wooden chair in the front row, sighed, texted my wife about "the stinker" sermon, and began to pray. Insecurity set in, as it often did directly after preaching, but I watched as students stayed. I watched Georges, a volunteer in the choir who soon would become a teammate during the wild sixteen days, sing along with passion. I'd planned a coffee meeting with an amazing young leader, Wes, but when the time to meet came, I texted him to grab his guitar and come to Hughes.

We stayed in Hughes, like a beautiful incubator for what God was doing, for hours and hours. Within hours, my phone began to blow up and I tried to respond...

"What is God doing?"

"We are still worshiping…" I texted back.

"Zach, have you heard about what's going down at Asbury?"

"Ha…well…yes. You need to get down here…" I sheepishly typed and pressed send.

Throughout the day, more students came. Faculty and leadership would come into Hughes with eyes wide, smiles on their faces, and start discussing the next steps. Pastors and friends from around the area came to see. My consistent reaction was a quiet giggle, a shrug of my shoulders, and usually a hug. I remember running into one campus leader I greatly respect and love, and I told him, "It's time to be bold, Mark. Be bold." Over the next sixteen days, Mark would become a dear comrade, a humble servant, and a secret weapon as he coordinated media, security, and really just about anything that was needed behind the scenes.

I had texted my mentor and dear friend Dr. David Thomas, whose research and writing is on the very subject of prayer that precedes revival and awakening. He lived just up the road, so he arrived a bit after dinner. I then found myself with him and some university leaders in the humble basement of Hughes Auditorium, where David said in his sweet and confident voice, "I think you might have something here. Might you consider keeping Hughes open through the night?"

I had absolutely no clue that the sermon I'd given earlier that morning, the one that felt quite lacking, would be the first sermon of sixteen days of a beautiful encounter with Jesus. I had no idea that that meeting in the Hughes basement would mean so much. There was no thought that these sixteen days would spur on moments and movements around college campuses, churches around the United States and abroad, igniting hearts to truly follow Jesus, experiencing His love and pouring it out on others. My life and my family would never be the same…

Later, a dear friend was asked to describe the chapel service that "launched" this supernatural experience and he replied, "It was ordinary and unremarkable…not bad but…"

How does it feel going viral for being ordinary and unremarkable? How do I feel being the one who preached a stinker that was a part of a move of God?

Humbling.

A HEADS-UP

If you've picked up this book to read my firsthand accounts of the Asbury Outpouring, you'll find much more than that. You'll find my thoughts, prayers, and ideas that were distilled for many years before February 8, 2023, and have been continuing since those wonderful sixteen days. You'll hear about this concept of *spiritual formation*, woven throughout each chapter, which is the journey of a Christ follower being shaped, transformed, and more and more reliant on the Spirit of God to resemble and represent Jesus Christ and His teaching. In *Invitation to a Journey*, M. Robert Mulholland Jr. beautifully defines it as "a process of being formed in the image of Christ for the sake of others."[1] This transformative process may be initiated by the Holy Spirit, Scripture, a sermon you hear, a conversation over coffee, or maybe (I earnestly pray) even this book. In the following pages, I hope you'll experience vulnerability and honesty in ways I have been—and am still being—formed, through the power of the Holy Spirit, into living more like Jesus Christ on a daily basis.

If there was a book of *prescriptive* steps to experience what happened on Asbury's campus, I would warn you to stay away from it. If there were an eloquently written book describing the 384 hours of continual prayer and worship during that time, it would probably be written by one of my gifted and anointed teammates...and I would cheer you on as you read it. But the book you've picked up is a vulnerable look at what I observed, what I have been exploring and pursuing and sharing with pretty much everyone since. It presents a way of pursuing and preparing for a fresh outpouring of God's spirit through an essential posture of humility.

My hope and prayer is that through these stories and the unpacking of ideas, the Spirit would confront pride in our lives and mold us into entrustable vessels for a fresh outpouring of His Spirit. A prideful disciple is a difficult tool for God to use and a sparkly church is not winning the next generation back to Christ. These truths also existed during Jesus' ministry and the early church too. But the sauce of Jesus and His ministry was His humility and His very real outworking of it.

You and I follow a God who radically humbled Himself for our sake. Yet for some reason, very few of us feel compelled to seek that same humility. Instead, we'd rather pursue other things deemed more winsome or effective like followers, platform, or washboard abs. Why don't we put all those things on the table, like we did for sixteen days at Asbury, and let God address them?

Are you up for doing the work that leads to looking more like Jesus by the end of this book? If being marked by Christlike humility is on the table, I am raising my hand and saying yes to the hard work of chasing after Christ and His humility.

Would you say yes with me?

Chapter 1

Going Lower

"Humility is too wonderful a thing for us
not to consider and pursue. It is like oxygen.
Humility is restorative, normalizing. It is for your
soul what a good night's sleep is for your body."

GAVIN ORTLUND

*"You know that those who are regarded as rulers of
the Gentiles lord it over them, and their high officials
exercise authority over them. Not so with you.
Instead, whoever wants to become great among you
must be your servant, and whoever wants to be first
must be slave of all. For even the Son of Man
did not come to be served, but to serve,
and to give his life as a ransom for many."*

JESUS, IN MARK 10:42–45

can be a prideful man, but I'm writing on humility.

You're asking, "Who is this guy? Who does he think he is to write a book on humility?"

I hear you, and I've asked the same questions. I feel uncomfortable...but compelled as well.

This is a bit awkward. If I had to guess, I'd guess you might be a wee bit prideful too.

But it's okay, it's okay. Let's stay at "the table," prayerfully in the conversation.

I know there are many aspects of this journey that will surprise us, like the beautiful lowliness of Jesus but also the icky, subtle, and religiously acceptable ways pride shows up in our lives. As we dive into this conversation, we must stay malleable and submitted...like clay on the potter's wheel (Isaiah 64:8).

Tim Keller wrote, "Humility is so shy, if you begin talking about it, it leaves." I read that with a bit of fear and trembling. I read that as a fragile jar of clay...a bit intimidated.

But we need to talk about humility...and we need to prioritize the pursuit of it.

During the Outpouring, I felt like a fragile jar of clay standing on that small, Christian university campus. I felt wrecked by the humility of God and His profound gentleness. His kindness, gentleness, simplicity, and humility fell on all of us who were present. We had no choice but to respond.

I may be an unlikely author for this book. Pride is something the Lord has convicted me of before, and has since the Outpouring, but I am captivated by Christ's loving humility and would love to invite you to chase Jesus and His humility with me. As we look toward this journey, I would like to share with you a definition for humility that we can unpack and discuss through this book: Humility is the simple and freeing agreement of the biblical assessment of who God is and who I am. It is rooted in our belovedness and adoption of the Father[1] so we aren't tricked into timidity or start feeling like a worm. This humility is walked out in friendship with Jesus,[2] relying on His example and grace when we falter and initiated and empowered by the Holy Spirit[3] because we could not do this by pure will or our own hard work.

BASE CAMP

When you set your mind on the peak of a mighty mountain, let's say Everest or K2, there is a season of preparation, study, and training. Not only do you prepare your lungs, legs, and mind to make the trek, you also gather a team of guides and comrades for the journey.

There are moments, amid the adventure preparation, when you decide the starting place, where you rest, regroup, and strategize for the next stretch. The base camp, where this all gets started, is a really significant place in the story of a mountaineer. This is the launch pad for the expedition upward.

We are now at a base camp, but before ascending, would we consider what might be waiting for us in the lower places, lower with Jesus? Culture, inside and outside of the Church, uses words like *ascend, climb, conquer*. Culture can cast a vision of trekking up your leadership mountain and planting that flag victoriously on the summit, like a boss. In Christendom, I have heard a disproportionate amount of teaching about going higher and higher with Jesus in worship, preaching, or prayer.

It feeds our desire to win, conquer, and so on, but we are invited as followers of Christ to go lower. *Lower* gets a bad rap...like we are going to lose character or morals. Descending makes me think of a sketchy basement or even hell.

One of my favorite places on earth is my sweet KP and my college friends' lake house. You have to climb a little hill and then after a gasp and pause to take in the beauty, you descend carefully down steep steps to one of the most beautiful and precious beaches I've ever enjoyed. So, instead of looking down creaky steps with a flickering light into an unfinished basement in a horror film, what if you see going lower as the careful walk lower into beauty. What if Jesus is waiting for us when we are going lower in humility?

Jesus challenges us to consider the concept of lower and all it entails in a short teaching in Luke 14, verses 7–11. Christ, in the home of a well-known religious leader, saw guests taking seats of honor possibly out of prideful ambition or posturing. Jesus confronts this with a parable about a wedding feast. At the feast, instead of calculating and posturing to get the best seat, which could result in being called out and embarrassed, He says to take the lowest seat at the table. Take the lowest seat and wait for the host to invite you to a more distinguished seat.

Jesus even uses the world *recline* or in some translations *lay back* when talking about the lowest seat. So many times (confession here), I might take the lowest seat but in no way is my posture or priority in those moments focused on reclining and lying back. I might be at the lowest seat, but I'm on the edge of my chair, eager to get invited "higher," eager to be noticed and thanked. I'm not settled and resting in the lowest seat totally confident in who I am and trusting the master to put me in the seat I need to be sitting in. How could we, while at "base camp," consider going to the lowest seat and rely on the master to invite us to a seat of honor? What if this sort of humility, straight out of the mouth of Jesus, was reclaimed by the Church today? This is a **radical humility**, or better defined, biblical humility.

What will it take to go lower? To enter the sweet depth of Jesus and all of who He is? *Enduring surrender, humble hunger, and vulnerable participation will be tested.* In *Mere Christianity*, C. S. Lewis speaks of these first steps: "If anyone would like to acquire humility, I can, I think, tell him the first step. The first step is to realize that one is proud. And a biggish step, too. At least, nothing whatever can be done before it. If you think you are not conceited, it means you are very conceited indeed."[4]

In the coming conversations we will need to take "biggish steps," beginning with how Christ's humility confronts us and reveals places in our lives that do not line up. We must go there first to start the journey toward lower. We then will explore the crucible journey of leading as Christians and share our wounds and discuss suffering in the crushing. Just like beginning a journey up Everest, we have to prepare, be ready, and then go. Let's dive into the first chapters with that same sort of intensity like the first steps up a peak.

Lord, give us enduring surrender...keep us on the potter's wheel, keep our egos on the altar, help us keep our minds and hearts surrendered during the hard, humbling work we are stepping into.

Lord, give us humble hunger...hunger to look more like You and fullness, not to claim it and flex how humble we have become (and negating our work) but a humble hunger for all that You have for us.

Jesus, we want to experience Your kindness, humility, and gentleness as we say "yes" to vulnerability, fragility, and a ready yes for what You want for us. Help us not self-protect but vulnerably participate in Your deep formation.

RADICAL HUMILITY

When Asbury University chapel did not end on February 8, I was not immediately concerned about being prideful. I was in awe of Jesus' tangible and gently powerful presence in the auditorium and did not want to be distracted. Jesus had met many of us in a profound way. The last words of my sermon flowed into honest worship. That authentic worship became hours of lingering, prayer, testimony, and much more. God's presence was in the auditorium in a powerful and sweetly simple way.

Early on, I was afraid this experience was going to be centered around a personality and move into pride. It took up a large amount of my thought life, and sadly, on one of the first nights of those days at Asbury, I decided to check social media to see if anyone was talking about Asbury. Before I knew it, the sun was rising...I had wandered down the tempting rabbit hole of social media posts, hashtags, shout-outs, and more. That night, the power and presence of God collided with my humanity, hubris, and hunger for affirmation from man. (Welcome to an authentic book from a fragile and hopeful man; I hope you don't put it down now.)

After that "all-nighter," I deleted multiple apps and asked my wonderful wife to handle much of what was going on with my phone. I repostured and refocused on what God was doing. But I will never forget the moment when someone casually mentioned that the sermon I preached had gone viral and millions of people had viewed the video from February 8. My stomach sank, my brain got tangled up, and concern rushed in. I will not lie...there were many times in my years of ministry when I had thought that "viral" would be pretty cool. But what God was doing in our midst was so antithetical to what was peeking its head over a horizon of going lower in my life. It was too special and too holy to be experienced on an app or a website. It was a moment of deep spiritual formation for me.

As the crowds grew, Asbury's administration warned us not to step outside without security or a friend, which felt so strange and uncomfortable...quite contradictory to some of my convictions about spiritual leadership. "Nameless and faceless" was what we said we wanted to be...but my name was "out there" and many people recognized my face. Our focus on "anti-celebrity culture" and the regular reminder that we were here for Jesus, the only "celebrity in the room," was prevalent. But at the same time, I started getting requests for interviews by big media outlets, and I was being offered opportunities to meet spiritual heroes who had come to see what God was doing. Had I become a celebrity of an "anti-celebrity movement"?

Pride puts our eyes on ourselves. During the days of the Asbury Outpouring, pride could sneak up and strike at any moment. Some moments meant wrangling with self and pride while intentionally submitting to Jesus. The Spirit's generosity, and the voice of many friends, would remind me of what walking in humility looks like. Those of us overseeing the Outpouring decided that we would hold no offense and would hold things open-handed. We would release every prerogative and agenda we might have for the sake of others and to the glory of

God. We were experiencing the fragility of following Jesus in ministry. I felt fragile; my ego and character felt fragile.

The Outpouring showed me that I *have to* intentionally pursue humility. It doesn't simply happen. Chasing the alternative, of self and pride, leads to dark and empty places.

It also showed me that my formation of humility and death to pride had started long before the Outpouring... when I felt broken, disappointed, and like unwanted rubbish.

GOOD SOIL

Do you know there is a difference between dirt and soil? Soil is what supports the growth of plants, while dirt—dirt collects by your front door or under your nails. Most of the time, when I see dirt, I brush it away because I see no need for it. We do this often with elements of our stories... brush them away, set them aside, and pay no attention because we see no possibility or potential in them. Dirt does not have potential. It cannot grow plants. But soil can. Our stories, *your story*, the specific moments and circumstances of story, are not dirt to brush away but, if cared for well, are soil for growth. If stewarded well, it's brimming with potential and possibility.

So how do you make really good soil? By adding a little compost.

Compost is a mixture of ingredients, usually organic kitchen scraps, yard waste, manure, and other discardable, organic things that when stewarded correctly cultivate nutrient-rich soil. This process can take as little as two weeks or possibly up to two years before the peak performing soil arrives. Ultimately, some of the richest soil that is the most poised for growth and brimming with potential could be made up of *trash*...or at least what we perceive as trash. Stinky, rotten, bothersome yuck. When I looked up *compost bins* on the internet, there was a wide range of types and prices; one even marketed itself as "transforming pretty much whatever you eat into nutrient-rich plant food with little to no smell or flies!" Who knew there was such a booming compost industry? To be honest, I did. I did because of my stepdad, Greg.

Greg was a garage door salesman from Texas who would pick me up most days after school (or at least I remember it this way) with a slightly frozen Dr Pepper. He also was the ultimate amateur gardener. He loved working in our backyard in Colorado Springs, Colorado. He made it an oasis with multiple trails, man-made ponds and streams, a hammock, a "bowling ball garden," and a beloved fire pit. Imagine being a third grader with your own log bridge over a creek or being a sixth grader with a sweet outdoor fireplace you can invite your friends over to sit around. The plants were lush, the garden was successful, and the architecture and style were funky and cool. The reality was that as we swayed in the hammock or got warm by the fire pit, we were experiencing the benefits of trash. Trash being repurposed and stewarded strategically by an intentional gardener. The flower beds had compost soil and the beloved fire pit had walls made of crumpled aluminum cans covered in stucco.

My mom and Greg had made multiple compost bins that sat on the side of the house. They provided unbelievable soil for their gardens. Those bins held high-growing-potential soil, but to me, they were full of my trash. Mom and Greg were pretty ruthless about not throwing away scraps, to the point that where I saw a banana peel, they saw soil, and when I made eggs and tossed shells away, they took them out of the trash can and put the shells into a bucket. <u>Where I saw trash, they saw potential. Nothing would be wasted because every-thing had potential.</u>

Scraps placed in the trash are just trash in a bin. But that trash, when handled with care and intentionality, can compost into something fertile and favored for growth. That lesson taught me that what I considered to be unworthy trash in my life could be turned into compost piles of good and bad stewarded by Jesus. It gave me a way to see who I was and who He is.

Perspective lets us accurately assess our good and bad. What we bring in brokenness and in our best, and through greater perspective our stories, we continue to contend for humility in our lives. Our stories, the good and bad, handled by the Great Gardener, can become some of the richest soil for the growth of Christ-likeness, which is a great place to begin our journey toward lower.

Our weakness, brokenness, hurts, and small offerings can all be stewarded by the Spirit to become compost in the richest soil where our humility can take root and grow. The key, as with many things, is in who is doing the gardening. Possibly you read this and rolled your eyes or are already tempted to skip ahead because you've heard this before or, praise God, your story does not seemingly resemble a trash heap. But each of our stories includes limits, experiences, and memories that can act as elements for good compost. Our stories, if submitted to the Lord, can be a place where greater humility can grow. Engaging our story with open eyes and hands can aid in the chase for humility.

THE POWER OF OUR STORY

On February 8, following a seemingly typical chapel service at Asbury University, we could tell God was meeting us in a unique way. My sermon had ended, somewhat abruptly, and I watched Gen Z students stay and worship and pray as the gospel choir led us in worship. As I was taking videos on my phone and processing the events via text with my wife, saying prayers and singing in between, others were beginning to stir. I will never forget the moments when college students sang out "I got joy down deep in my soul" and my friend Georges danced and sang with his guitar. Georges would lead worship for approximately twelve hours straight on the first day.

In these hours of worship, often with no lyrics but with lively participation, Asbury's chaplain and I were approached by a student leader on campus named Charlie. I was a guest speaker, so I did not know Charlie well or his story but would soon hear it, feel it, and have the chance to pray and cheer him on in sharing it. It was one of the first "formalized" moments after I left the stage that day.

Charlie told a raw and authentic story that pointed to Christ with vulnerability, almost like a gentle invite to his peers to "go ahead...tell your story...let's go there." Charlie's story began a cascading effect of testimonies that seemed to truly be fertilizer to what God was planting and growing. Vulnerability and honesty were mixed with hope and vision. Stories became not only a regular practice during our sixteen days at Asbury but a necessity to participate with what God was doing in our midst.

The stories of many Gen Z men and women rang out often from the stage—from suicidal ideation, abuse, porn addiction, and grief over death to experiencing provision and healing. A breathtaking moment early in the Outpouring happened when a student yelled out, "NO ONE SEES ME!" Almost immediately, like a guard dog that would not allow Satan to lie to this girl, another woman yelled back, with almost equal fervor, "WE SEE YOU!" Women from all over the chapel got up and surrounded this brave young testifier, praying and being present with her. I can't write about this moment without crying.

This story, and many others, oriented individuals and the community to Jesus. Our stories can do the same. All of these things were shared and became the compost for God to move. God moved through all of these elements, good and bad, to give us rich soil. Rich soil was not made by the efforts and heroism of the ones telling them but of the God they were testifying about. Radical humility and stories became tied together. We knew who we were, where we came from, what we were longing for, and who would be the provider. The story became our reorienting tool to remind us that there was only one hero of this story, only one celebrity of the moment, and that person was Jesus.

MY COMPOST STORY

My desire is to be one of the most grateful people you've ever met. I have already given up being the brightest or most poetic author you've ever read, the most captivating preacher, the most strategic and impressive leader, and other things I strove for and desired for sadly too long in my own journey. I do believe that if I pursue gratitude, humility expressed outwardly, it'll keep me in the sweet spot. I am fully aware of my brokenness, failures, and trauma. I have become strangely comfortable with grief. In all of these circumstances, though, I am very aware of where I could be, what I deserve, and what I am capable of, and how generous and gracious Jesus is. As I type this sentence (literally the last nineteen letters), I am shocked that I get to write a book. Here is why...

I grew up Jewish and had never heard of the Gospel. I had once watched the musical *Jesus Christ Superstar* and had dabbled in a couple VeggieTales movies but only at a certain family's home. My family lived out our faith to the best of our ability: going to synagogue, celebrating most of the festivals and holidays, training and participating in Bar Mitzvahs, and my mom even came and taught our elementary school classes about Hanukkah when all my friends just could not wait for winter (some would call it Christmas) break. It became more difficult when we moved west, away from our family on the East Coast, to Colorado Springs.

Along this faith journey, I was also introduced to sexual brokenness. Some of my earliest memories are of my perpetrator and me. Those memories and the immense shame and guilt tied to those experiences are still topics of conversation in counseling and with my gentle yet fierce wife.

Brokenness, disappointments, divorces, and splintered relationships complicated things for me and I began to wonder a lot about manhood, identity, my sexuality, and more. I wrestled with the simple questions, "Do I have what it takes?" and "Am I uniquely delighted in and loved?" These were two key questions that I asked then and continued to wrestle with over the years. The "trash" was piling up. Yet I hadn't heard a hint toward the composting work of the Gospel. I hadn't ever met the Great Composter of my yuck, Jesus. I covered up my confusion and brokenness with overachieving, extraversion, and the thought that my religion would ultimately cover that pain somehow (although I was not very faithful to Hebrew school).

My rabbi had cast a vision that things would improve at my Bar Mitzvah. My story did pivot at my Bar Mitzvah, or at least I thought it did, but in ways much different than expected. I'd worked hard, crying the week before over fear that I would not remember my Torah portion for my big day. When the day arrived, I received tons of gifts and had a lavish party with a DJ, a caricature artist, and good food...but I did not feel better. I did not feel whole. It just felt like a religious event layered upon some immense hurt and brokenness. I don't think I ever returned to synagogue after my Bar Mitzvah. And after thirteen or so years of covering my hurt, I found something else to help—drugs, alcohol, and girls. My coping mechanisms only led to other types of hurt, *but* there was one thing that felt like a relief in a substantial way: soccer.

I was not really all that good, but in that game, I found a place of belonging. Not only had I found a place of belonging, but I also started to take notice of some of the relationships off the field between fathers and their sons. I noticed families leaning in and loving my mom and me by helping me with rides, meals, and more. Through this, I got a glimpse into how these fathers loved their sons and served their families. I would just watch and watch these fathers like I was paparazzi. Doug, Jeff, Jim, Dave, Ralph, and Ken were dads who embodied the Gospel to me through their love for their families. I noticed that the common theme in all of these men's lives was that they prayed before dinner. Now, I did not grow up praying before dinner, but I had heard of this before. Some of these dads would even say, "In Jesus' name, amen." These men who loved so well were all Christians. I especially noticed their love for their sons on my teams, and their sons played soccer differently. They weren't exceptionally better than all the others, but they exuded something I didn't. This led to me saying yes to an invitation to a teammate's basement for what I thought was a party one night.

I walked down into Mason's basement to find myself at my high school's Fellowship of Christian Athletes (FCA). To my surprise, there was no weed or alcohol at this party, just a guitar, djembe, singing, and a short testimony shared by a man named Dave. Dave shared many things, I am sure, but I remember basically only one thing: He is a Father to the fatherless and He puts lonely people in families. This one verse, from Psalm 68, captivated and convicted me. I cried. Hard. I hid in the corner as I listened and got real snotty. And then I came to my secular senses...

"I can't believe this junk! They've tricked me. I need to leave."

I spooked and left. But I was so curious that I asked my friend Jeff for a Bible and to meet me at Starbucks to process. I asked hard questions about hell, hurt, and Hitler (the trifecta), and Jeff was courageous and clear. I heard the Gospel again, clearly. I then dove into several Bible studies and went to services on Sundays at a new church plant. FCA, that meeting at Starbucks, and diving into these communities and experiences began my journey of meeting Jesus. A year later, I gave my life to Jesus and asked Him to lead me for the rest of my life. There were many things that I would have to work on and pursue healing for, but I was adopted. I was His. I had experienced Him and knew the best news ever. For that, I would be forever grateful, and to the best of my ability, would chase after Him for the rest of my life.

Since surrendering my life to Jesus when I was sixteen years old, I have experienced tremendous brokenness and deep disappointment. I've also experienced extravagant grace and life-changing encounters with God. For that, I am deeply thankful...I am confident that He makes flower beds from my trash. Some of the best fruit and growth in my life has sprouted from the soil of my suffering and failures. He is the Master Gardener and artful at compost.

THOUGH FORMERLY I WAS A _____

Possibly no man, other than Jesus, has had a greater impact on the Christian faith than the apostle Paul. He is the ultimate example of God cultivating trash into fertile soil. Paul was confronted by Christ and realized quickly that Christ would use all of Paul's life, messes and mastery, for His own formation and leading the Church. Stories of redemption from Saul's murderous threats to becoming a radical church planter and teacher not only rippled through churches and conversations of the early Church but in our preaching and conversations today. The fruit from Paul's compost is still planting seeds today.

Later in Paul's ministry, he radically invested himself in an apprentice named Timothy to whom he entrusted a group of churches in Ephesus (modern-day Turkey). In a letter to his apprentice Timothy, Paul shares how his own story has been used by the Spirit for forming him into a man who is grateful and humbly aware.

Even though I was once a blasphemer and a persecutor and a violent man, I was shown mercy because I acted in ignorance and unbelief. The grace of our Lord was poured out on me abundantly, along with the faith and love that are in Christ Jesus.

Here is a trustworthy saying that deserves full acceptance: Christ Jesus came into the world to save sinners— of whom I am the worst. But for that very reason I was shown mercy so that in me, the worst of sinners, Christ Jesus might display his immense patience as an example for those who would believe in him and receive eternal life. (1 Timothy 1:13–16)

How often do we utilize our story to capture a room or woo an individual, all as a humblebrag on what we've accomplished? Because of Paul's profound awareness of where he had been and where he was headed, his story can be used in more poignant ways. Paul's life was compost that God used for transformation: Saul, trash, to Paul, growth and humble apostolic leadership.

Paul shared things that many of us would want to hide or toss out, but he shared them as a profound witness to the power of Christ's mercy and love. This is not worm theology, self-deprecation to get a giggle, but a step of radical humility for Christ's glory. Paul would tell his story often and point to the harm he had done as a Pharisee, both of which were used as compost for His new calling and platform.

Let's pause before we move ahead and try a practice that allows Scripture to address us, possibly confronting and revealing new things for us to consider, rest in, and possibly celebrate:

- Though formerly I was a _____
- I was shown (what did you experience from Jesus?)
  _____

- Because I (what were you caught in? Living in?)
  _____

- The grace of the Lord was poured out abundantly upon me, along with (what else did you experience?) _____

Paul says, *Here is a trustworthy saying that deserves full acceptance: Christ Jesus came into the world to save sinners—of whom I am the worst. But for that very reason I was shown mercy so that in me, the worst of sinners, Christ Jesus might display his immense patience as an example for those who would believe in him and receive eternal life.*

- How can you relate to this? What might Jesus display through your example?

How does that feel? Anytime I do this practice I am more grateful and deeply humbled. Your story, when placed in context of Christ's story and mission, will lead you to greater humility and gratitude.

A GOING LOWER PRACTICE—YOUR STORY

As we chase humble, might we start at the simple launching pad of ourselves? My story is the soil that the Gardener is churning up, fertilizing, pruning out of, and more.

I write out my testimony once a week as a regular weekly practice in my life. I wonder if you might start exploring your own story through the questions below and see if it might offer opportunities for greater perspective, for ways to grow in gratitude for His provision and work in your life, or to develop greater self-awareness (your strengths and shadows), and possibly even process and grieve difficult memories. Just months ago, doing this practice, I exploded in new gratitude for the memory of a friend who was instrumental in introducing me to Jesus that I had honestly forgotten over the years. I was humbled that God had pursued me by a sweet friend in elementary school and his faithful family's expression of Christ's love. I have also been surprised by elements of my story that I've clung to in bitterness or anger that I was able to release for greater formation. It's a simple practice, no rocket science here, but it has been exponentially impactful in my own pursuit of greater humility and Christ-like character.

- Before Christ—What was life like for you before meeting Christ?
- Meeting Christ—How did you meet Jesus and come to give your life over to Him?
- Since Christ—What has life been like since relinquishing your life and following Jesus?
- Experiencing Christ—What is the latest encounter or thing you've learned from Jesus?
- Desiring Christ—What is one way you want to experience God by the next time you tell your story?

section one

Forming Humility

Chapter 2

Confrontation

"God is opposed to the proud,
but gives grace to the humble."

JAMES 4:6 (NASB), QUOTING PROVERBS 3:34

"It is always better to have an awkward
conversation before an awkward situation."

MY YOUTH PASTOR,
TALKING ABOUT DATING GIRLS

*O*kay, awkward conversation. My editor mentioned that kicking off my first book with the wonderful topic of confrontation might be a bit crazy. But I could not start this conversation without acknowledging that as we pursue humility, we will be confronted. The world today hates this word, doesn't it? Probably because we do not know how to do it well. We are clunky and clumsy (or worse) in confrontation.

This book and this conversation are not for me to confront you. Who am I to do that? I am continually being confronted myself. The one who will be confronting us, if we lean in throughout these chapters, is (I pray) God in three parts: our Advocate and Comforter, the Spirit; the gentle and humble Jesus; and our fierce Father in heaven. Our job is to stay in it, to become more like Jesus through His gentle and constructive confrontation and respond accordingly.

Some things are like an itchy sweater or a pebble in your shoe. They're subtle and annoying so you can't ignore them. They eventually require action. I ended that Asbury chapel service with this simple prayer: "I pray that this sits on you like an itchy sweater...that you have to itch."

It seemed that He answered, as students stayed in the chapel to worship. On that day, the itchiness came from Romans 12 describing God's authentic love.

Christ's kindness, gentleness, and humility confront me daily and I do my best to respond, like scratching an itch from an itchy sweater. This might be that I am short with my daughter as she takes 167 years (possibly an exaggeration) to get ready for school. Like an itchy sweater, Christ's kindness collides with mine and calls me to respond differently. Christ's gentleness confronts me, like a pebble in my shoe, when I'm in an airport and someone pushes me aside to snag their Frappuccino. I am confronted by His humility right now as I rattle through hundreds of examples I could use to make this point of my deep need to be addressed and transformed more into Christ-likeness in everyday life.

I pray that it might do the same to you. When you are leading in your vocation, when you are responding to less than desirable service at a restaurant, or you are putting your child to bed... might Christ's humility be present and keep us attentive to our own formation and the opportunity to share in His humility?

ITCHY SWEATERS AND "GREENROOMS"

One "itchy sweater" that arose during those sixteen days was consecration. We were intentionally setting aside or apart for God's special use. Like tools for a surgery being especially cleaned or separated for the important work they'd soon to be used for, we embraced consecration through the hard but important work of getting right with Jesus and by resting in the Spirit's power and Jesus' work on the cross for the work ahead.

The days at Asbury were uniquely impactful and intense. In Hughes Auditorium, God's presence was so palpably thick that His kindness led us to repentance. Many testified to feeling it as soon as they stepped through the precipice of one of the chapel's doors, but there was a greater epicenter in what we called the "consecration room," a room specifically for those who were preparing to step out in front of the worshippers. This room prioritized space to prepare through confession, prayer, and worship.

Early on during the Outpouring, several of my teammates were facilitating twenty-four-hour worship and we began running out of worship leaders. In response, the team began to prophetically identify worshippers through riskful prayer: We would need a drummer, pray for the Spirit to highlight a drummer, then go ask the man or woman God pointed out if they played drums. Praise God that this worked a majority of the time. *It was almost like Jesus was in charge or something.*

Because we did not know these new friends, we chose a room upstairs in Hughes Auditorium to be a place to prepare for stepping up onstage. Many churches have and utilize these places, or greenrooms, before events as a place to breathe, regroup, maybe snack, all before getting up onstage. This room became our consecration room.

Note, though, that I'm not saying that greenrooms are evil, nor do they need to all be replaced by consecration rooms. A rearranged, dimly lit greenroom with a new title does not make a consecration room. Hunger, the pursuit of purity, confession, and prioritization do.

If Asbury's chapel was palpable with God's peace and presence, the consecration room was thick, like molasses, with Jesus' holy, kind, confrontational presence. It was a requirement that worship leaders and speakers would spend time in this room for at least thirty minutes before getting onstage. Often these thirty-minute sessions would run over because of the work Christ was doing in and through the teams facilitating the room and preparing to lead during the Outpouring. There were multiple times that I would finish sharing or facilitating, but as we stepped back into corporate worship, we'd have no worship band because they were still experiencing worship, prayer, confrontation, and pushing through frustration to land in consecration. It was and is holy. Those were some of the most precious moments of my sixteen days, not the stage or meeting wonderful new friends but confrontation and consecration set aside for the Lord's work.

You are probably not about to step onstage to preach or lead worship during a unique outpouring that is drawing the world's attention, but what if you pushed through confrontation to honest and authentic consecration? What would it look like to consecrate our iPhones? Consecrate laptops? Consecrate our streaming services? Our wallets? Consecrate our calendars? I recently learned that the historic Crusaders, before going out on their "mission," would be baptized but hold their swords up and out of the water so their bodies, hearts, and minds would be set aside in the act of baptism but their hand and sword would not be. This gave them the "right" to do what they would with the sword and not be confronted because that part of their life had not died to self like baptism represents. Could you imagine the spirit-filled Crusader wrestling with the rhythms of confrontation that they experienced? Doesn't that image confront you? How many times do we identify with Christ's humility, His death, His burial, and His resurrection while "holding" our wallet, iPhone, career, or whatever might be preferred over the water of baptism? Could we allow ourselves to be confronted by the Truth of Jesus and His Gospel? Can we endure the rhythm of confrontation so that we might be seen more in His image... exuding His humility?

BLUE CHAIRS

When you enter my home in Lexington, Kentucky, you see a blue chair in the corner of the living room, with a side table, lamp, and a candle next to it. This blue chair is where I meet with Jesus, usually in my devotional time or in processing my day. The journey toward humility did not begin in that blue chair, but over the last couple years, it might be the most poignant place to process and pursue Jesus and His character in my life. It hasn't been an altar, stage, or conference breakout session, but an ordinary blue chair we ordered online. Isn't that a bit like how Jesus works?

We don't need a tabernacle, just a surrendered kitchen table. We don't always need an altar or throne room, just a chair in the corner of a messy living room.

The process of humility takes spending time with capital *H* Humble, and His name is Jesus. The significance of a space like this blue chair is that it is set apart for conversation with Jesus. If I want to look more like Jesus, I need to create a space where I humble myself and let Him address me, all of me, and submit myself to His formation in my life. It's like a personal trainer. If you are not in the gym and not humble enough for your trainer to correct how you are lifting, eating, stretching, and so on… how beneficial is it to have a personal trainer? It just looks cool or feels better to have one, but you won't actually benefit at all. So many of us live this way with Jesus and miss out on interacting with Him and the transformation that takes place in our lives by following Him. So, as I sit in that blue chair, I allow Christ to be in charge.

Where do you sit regularly with Jesus and allow Him to confront and comfort you in your journey?

WRESTLING WITH GOD

When you spend time with God, is your experience ever like a sweaty wrestling match? Sometimes my mind feels like I'm being suplexed or my heart is twisting and turning. There is a powerful story in the Old Testament that depicts this. In Genesis 32:22–31, a man named Jacob had sent his family to go ahead on their journey and something peculiar occurred: He was confronted by a man who initiated a wrestling match. This "man" is understood to be God, Christ incarnate. This is a great picture of godly confrontation with the man initiating the wrestling, but like Jacob not letting go, us as disciples persevering for all that God has for us. Jacob, the son of Issac and grandson of Abraham, had heard stories of God moving and forming his ancestors through a wide variety of moments of confrontation with Him. Although this wrestling was different from others he had heard of in the past, like Abraham's journey to a land he did not know[1] or the potential sacrifice of his son Isaac,[2] Jacob was not going to waste this confrontation. He held on for a blessing that presented a greater identity, a new name, because Jacob understood the potential in the confrontation.

Then the man said, "Let me go, for day is breaking."
But Jacob said, "I will not let You go unless You declare a blessing on me.[3]

The man blessed Jacob with the new name. More than a cool nickname or catchy social media handle, a "new name" meant a refreshed identity. Jacob was renamed Israel[4] to show that his struggle was seen, dignified, and would mark him forever. What if there is a new name or deeper understanding of your identity waiting for you after confrontation, after the wrestling? Resilient, faithful, full of integrity, authentic...what might it be?

Maybe this story really resonates with the circumstances you are going through. Perhaps your marriage has been difficult and your spouse is leaning away when you are holding on, wrestling for formation and a new name spoken over your relationship. Possibly it's a wayward son or daughter and you're pushing through the confrontation, holding on to the hope of looking more like Jesus by the end of it. Maybe it is the challenge of leading a church or something more private like a desperate sin cycle. All of us are in a wrestling match. On repeat.

Let's not waste the confrontation.

Confrontation is hard and often we shy away from it. We don't see potential. *We see pain.* We don't see it ripe for new identity *but for potential new injuries.* In this story of Jacob wrestling, there was a cost—Jacob was left with a wrenched hip. Confrontation can come with a cost, but it also comes with a promise, like Jacob's new name and all it entailed. Is the cost worth the promise of formation to you? To us? With God, wrestling in and through confrontation brings us into greater Christ-likeness.

Confrontation is ripe with formation.

Being confronted with entitlement in a particular situation and leaning into it rather than scoffing at it can lead to greater freedom and humility. Being confronted with insecure striving is difficult but can actually lead to a new name like "confidently secure and settled." These are two examples from my quiet time this morning...not hypotheticals. My hip hurts, though.

CONFRONTING OUR PRIDE

Invitation to a Journey, by M. Robert Mulholland Jr., talks about the work of formation that occurs acutely at the point of our unlikeness to Christ. In this book, we'll look at formation occurring at our points of pride and entitlement. Mulholland sets it up:

> The process of being formed in the image of Christ takes place primarily at the point of our unlikeness to Christ's image...God is there, in grace, offering us the forgiveness, the cleansing, the liberation, the healing we need to begin the journey toward our wholeness and fulfillment in Christ...
>
> This means that one of the first dynamics of holistic spiritual formation will be confrontation. Through some channel—the Scripture, worship, a word of proclamation, the agency of a brother or sister in Christ, even the agency of an unbeliever—the Spirit of God may probe some area in which we are not formed in the image of Christ. That probing will probably always be confrontational, and it will always be a challenge and a call to us in our brokenness to come out of the brokenness into wholeness in Christ.[5]

Woof. *Probing and confrontation.* Are we still down to chase humility? The confrontation diagnoses where our inner selves and external actions do not line up with that of Christ Jesus. Like pieces of paper laid upon one another, with a matching image that you have to tweak and align just right, formation is the process of God's Spirit and our "yes" orienting our lives and actions with the image we desire to match. Imagine an image of Christ and all of His characteristics somehow lying on top of, or projected onto, a profile of our own characteristics and actions. What would stick out?

So, what happens if we see that the confrontation does not line up, and we do not want to surrender or be consecrated? This is, for example, like a follower of Jesus caught and confronted in lust who could choose consecration and take steps toward accountability, surrendering certain apps or screen time, for example, to push through for greater Christ-likeness. But the disciple chooses frustration and continues doing what led to confrontation in the first place. Though His power is made perfect in our weakness, we can still pursue and press on.

Honestly, many times in my blue chair, I'm confronted and I tap out and don't do the work, only to be confronted again at another time. The next time might be something seemingly less "spiritual," like not being able to find my keys, my seven-year-old not listening, or feeling overwhelmed by the amount of emails I have waiting for me. Though Christ is fully engaged in our formation, He is also kind, like a gentleman, and won't force it on us. When we are confronted, let's say in our pride or entitlement, we have two general choices: *consecration* or *frustration*.

Consecration is "setting apart or aside for specific use," as certain tools were consecrated for work in the temple in Scripture or men and women are consecrated or ordained in certain roles even today. Consecration following confrontation can act as a release and submission to Christ's transforming work in our lives.

Frustration usually shows up as avoidance or excuses, and it most likely will result in a repeated confrontation. This leads to feeling defeated and many have lost out on experiencing the power of the Spirit moving in their pursuit of holiness because they respond in frustration over and over again. I believe this is one of the many elements that has led to the exodus of my generation and younger from the Church. Confrontation is hard. Consecration is even harder. Frustration does not always feel like the intentional choice of throwing your arms up *but* possibly internally ignoring the Spirit or picking the more convenient, less sacrificial, choice.

The choice of frustration sends us reeling back to where we might have been before but we are more raw and...well, frustrated. This rhythm of frustration in the face of confrontation can lead to a very deflating and discouraging journey. One passage that depicts frustration, and thus the "great de-churching," is 2 Timothy 4:3–5. Paul writes to warn his young apprentice of a time that is coming. I believe we are in such a time, both culturally and often more personally in our formation.

For the time will come when people will not put up with sound doctrine. Instead, to suit their own desires, they will gather around them a great number of teachers to say what their itching ears want to hear. They will turn their ears away from the truth and turn aside to myths. But you, keep your head in all situations, endure hardship, do the work of an evangelist, discharge all the duties of your ministry.

There can be times when our belief is confronted by what the Bible says, which catalyzes an opportunity to steward confrontation and choose a new thing or clinging to our own thinking. I see this occur often on issues like gender and sexuality, what God really says about money, the cost of sin, or the exclusivity of Christ. These moments lead us to choose either frustration and disengaging or submitting to Biblical Truth and being formed by it.

Verse 5 uses the word *endure,* which means persisting even under stress. Imagine someone bench-pressing or carrying a heavy weight. Paul is depicting this person offloading that heavy weight for something lighter, or giving up the heavy weight of sound doctrine, which is true, and replacing it with another doctrine that does not require as much strength and fortitude. This lighter weight may be a doctrine that dwells very privately in us. A thought we have, an act we do, or a conviction we have that, when confronted by sound doctrine, leaves us with a choice...either lean into humble consecration or fold our arms in frustration. In that moment we can rest in what matches our own desires and even find a teacher (YouTube video, social media post/influencer, book) who will match us in a way that scratches our "itching ears." I could, right now as I am writing these words, find a YouTube video that would relieve me from being confronted by something I am wrestling with. I know of multiple social media influencers who would lessen the load, relieve me from "putting up with" difficulty, and make my life a lot easier. But I won't do that...I can't do that. My life is not my own and I'm placing myself before Jesus to be confronted, in humility, because I don't know better, so that I might look a bit more like Him at bedtime tonight.

The reality of formation, the work in our "blue chairs," is that even when we consecrate and push through for deeper formation, we will inevitably arrive back at confrontation because we will have that "unlikeness" to Christ again. Each time, we experience greater freedom, healing, and transformation.

When I was little, I received a rock polisher for Hanukkah, which rumbled rocks (mostly ones I found in my front yard) around, chipping off imperfections, smoothing edges, and making the stones purchased at Home Depot by my dad look like rocks you buy at a gift store. Like that rock polisher, the journey of spiritual formation in everyday life can feel like this: repetitive confrontations. Ultimately this is the journey of apprenticing with Jesus and for our conversation, the process of chasing humility (among all other characteristics of Jesus we desire). This process requires humility but has the potential to accelerate self-awareness and gratitude for Jesus. The reality is that the core of our spiritual journey, even at the very beginning of surrendering for our salvation, is humility. And humility remains vital in the posture and priority in our journey with Jesus.

JESUS' HUMILITY CONFRONTS ALL PRIDE

To talk about confrontation without clarity or compassion is dangerous. With the wrong confrontations, we are damaged and compromised, but with Christ's confrontations, we are healed and conformed into His image.

Many of us have been confronted in the name of Jesus or with many churchy phrases and it has felt more like bullying than Christ convicting and interacting with our broken and unformed parts. Some of us have been inundated with religious jargon or have struggled with the expectations of someone who doesn't align with the heart of Christ that we have retreated from the very concept of formation... possibly even from following Jesus. Sometimes this harsh, negative confrontation not aligned with Christ's heart or saturated with the Spirit stirs up damages and discourages. Instead of becoming more integrated and aligned to Jesus, we become disintegrated and confused.

This unhealthy confrontation can come from surprising or seemingly religious people who, like the Pharisees in the New Testament, are confronting people left and right with religion. In Matthew 23, Jesus confronted the Pharisees' incorrect types of confrontations, calling out the religious elite for hypocritically projecting such things on their listeners.

A prayer for those who have experienced this...

Jesus, would You reveal the corrupted and hypocritical confrontations in our lives, possibly those even tainted and tarnished by religious jargon or Christianese, that made us pursue lesser things than You and Your fullness.

Confrontation

We don't want to turn away from You when You, in Your gentle and humble ways, are confronting our brokenness and sin, but many of us have been battered by lesser and man-made confrontations that leave us feeling tender and confused.

Some of these harmful confrontational woes were keeping people out of the Kingdom (Matthew 23:13), leading them into hypocritical religious works (Matthew 23:15), on their "spiritual blindness" (Matthew 23:16–17), on tithing and generosity (Matthew 23:23), and then further confrontations on hypocrisy in the fifth, sixth, and seventh woes. Beautifully, Jesus uses the image of a dish tediously cleaned on the outside but left dirty on the inside in Matthew 23:25. This image is the exact opposite of what we desire Jesus to do in us. We do not just want Jesus to scrub us on the outside so we look all good and Christlike, but really confront what is inside us and transform us to be more like Christ. When Christ does this on the inside, it will inevitably be expressed on the outside. Have you experienced something like this before? Maybe painted with "Christian colors" but still so other-than. I want to pause, right here, and pray for you and for those who have been "confronted wrongly."

Heal us from unauthorized confrontations so that we can stand up tall in Your clear and transformational confrontations for the sake of our formation, transformation into Your likeness, and our witness to the world. Would we rest in Your clear but pointed probing and confrontation so that we might look more like You by bedtime, Lord. Amen.

Jesus' teachings, His actions and reactions—His very being—are confrontational. It is not what the world of His day nor the world and culture of today expects of God incarnate. Jesus is the best version of anything you could possibly fathom *but* probably different than you ever dreamed. This reality is confrontational to those looking at Jesus and experiencing Him in His fullness. To talk about Christian humility and form that sort of lowliness in us, we must look at Jesus in His fullness. I believe this begins in Philippians 2.

> *Have the same mindset as Christ Jesus: Who, being in very nature God, did not consider equality with God something to be used to His own advantage; rather, He made Himself nothing by taking the very nature of a servant, being made in human likeness. And being found in appearance as a man, He humbled Himself by becoming obedient to death—even death on a cross. Therefore God exalted Him to the highest place and gave Him the name that is above every name, that at the name of Jesus every knee should bow, in heaven and on earth and under the earth, and every tongue acknowledge that Jesus Christ is Lord, to the glory of God the Father.*

This, in some settings (usually ones with rich mahogany desks, leather-bound books, and/or stained-glass windows and pews), is called the Kenosis passage or the Kenotic Hymn. That funky word, *kenotic/kenosis*, stands for the profound action we see in verse 7: Christ's emptying. Christ's radical humility is depicted in these seven verses. In Jesus' act of kenosis, we see Him taking steps lower, resulting in His death on the cross following His exaltation by God the Father.

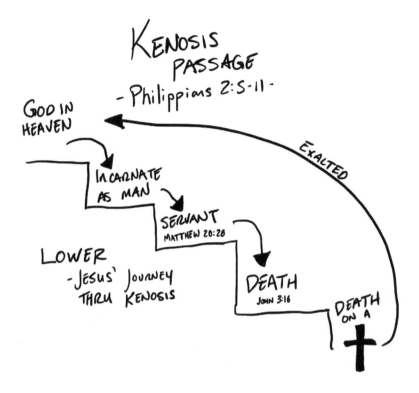

These seven verses may be some of the most confrontational verses in all of Scripture. Let's unpack them.

"BEING IN THE VERY NATURE OF GOD"

Christ was not bragging or flexing but simply resting in what He knew to be true from the beginning of time. He was and is God and though He emptied Himself of something, it was not His essence...His deity. This is a mystery but worth settling into as we consider Christ's confidence and humility. Jesus knew who He was and from that place of security, His Father could send His Son to serve those His heart broke for (John 3:16), to not reign over in power but love with a new understanding of power. We see this security and rightful and submitted confidence in who He is and what His purpose is throughout Jesus' life, not shying away or downplaying His deity, but serving and living humbly out of His identity.

In Luke 2:46–50, Jesus was found among teachers in the temple courts listening and asking questions. We cannot imagine this as a snot-nosed know-it-all poking around but a humble preteen Jesus, God incarnate in a young man's body (Voice breaking? Pimples? Little mustache arriving?), standing up, confident in who He was and is. Jesus shows this when he addresses His parents in verse 49, *"'Why were you searching for me?' he asked. 'Didn't you know I had to be in my Father's house?'"*

This same security and consecrated confidence is found in John 10 and John 13. In John 10, we see Christ's understanding of His identity and authority as He teaches, *"No one takes it from me, but I lay it down of my own accord. I have authority to lay it down, and I have authority to take it up again. This charge I have received from my Father"* (John 10:18, ESV). A very simple and short verse in John 13, before the heroically humble work of washing feet as God in flesh, also speaks of this: *"Jesus, knowing that the Father had given all things into his hands, and that he had come from God and was going back to God"* (John 13:3, ESV). Being in the very nature of God, Jesus knew where He had come from, what authority He had, and where He was headed. His identity was settled so deeply in His heart.

Over the last year, I have found myself in places that are so tempting to be who I am *not* because of the people I am meeting and serving alongside. I want to be smarter, funnier, more cool…It's ugly but true. The more rooted I am in who I am, being fully myself, the greater chance I have to act the way I desire: in humility.

How might confidence in your identity aid in your Christ-like humility?

"DID NOT COUNT EQUALITY WITH GOD AS SOMETHING TO BE GRASPED"

Have you ever had to "white-knuckle" cling to something? What about to a relationship? What about to something you have earned that seems to be slipping away? I often am tempted to scratch and claw for meaning in places I feel unseen or forgotten. I have felt like I have to fight for "space" at the table when the very seat I have was given and held for me by Jesus.

White-knuckling, claiming right, gripping, and clinging to these things are all appropriate for Jesus, the King of Kings, to do in light of who He is. In the throne room, there is "holy, holy, holy is the Lord God Almighty, who was, and is, and is to come" on repeat! The twenty-four elders that we read about in Revelation 4 also do not cling to their crowns but cast them at the foot of Jesus, worship, and say, "You are worthy, our Lord and God, to receive glory and honor and power, for you created all things, and by your will they were created and have their being" (Rev. 4:11). All of this is just a small portion of what Jesus could grasp and cling to in beautiful humility and sacrifice. His fingers did not curl around things He was unwilling to release: *He relinquished the things that could be flexed or presented for His own gain and comfort because of His unhindered love for us and desire to come, incarnate, to live among us and save us.*

In humility, He pursued and clung to us, dying on a cross for us, instead of sitting back and clinging to the throne of which He was fully deserving. If Christ were to come to earth today, He would put Himself in eight billionth place, placing everyone before Himself instead of where He deserves...first priority. The radical humility of this verse leads to the action of verse 7 in which He empties Himself. Like a very poignant cause and effect, we must understand the root of His actions.

This impactful humility would have been sung about in the early Church as these verses were understood to be a hymn in those days. Could you imagine if we sang of this radical humble release of rights, reputation, entitlement, agenda...if we would sing of this beautiful humility, how would that form us?

What are you tempted to white-knuckle cling to that you might loosen your grip of, and entitlement to, to pursue greater Christ-like humility?

"BUT EMPTIED HIMSELF"

Our achievements, roles, and titles all carry some sort of responsibility and benefit. An academic degree brings honor and respect for someone's expertise. A certain job, role, or title can lead to a fair, or extravagant, compensation. Many of us are focused on pursuing these sorts of things and when we reach them, we cling to them so tightly that they become distracting. It can be tempting to use them, like playing a hand in poker, for the sake of personal gain or influence.

I even think of this as I watch my seven-year-old, Eden, play tag on the playground. She sprints past the tagger, plants her feet on "the base," and flexes through sticking out her tongue and doing a little booty shake because she wants them to know what she accomplished and where she is at now. These things are not evil; I love my daughter deeply. I have achievements and degrees, and I am sure you have similar ones. But how do we steward and carry these?

We may not be playing tag and bragging about being on base, but how often do we flex certain achievements and results or compensation? Jesus had a right to present these sorts of things, like Eden on base at her playground, but He released, emptied, made void. He emptied Himself of this for the sake of others…for you and me. *Instead of clinging for His own gain, He released it all for the sake of you and me.*

Jesus did not remove His divine nature but rather took on the form of fully human, as a servant to the point of death. Matthew Poole beautifully depicts this activity as follows, "*Even as a king, by laying aside the tokens of his royalty, and putting on the habit of a merchant, when all the while he ceaseth not to be a king, or the highest in his own dominions.*"[6]

The activity of "kenos," kenosis, is the humbling activity of Jesus' incarnation. This sort of emptying was required for Him to come in fullness and minister to us. This very reality is also why He was misunderstood and even missed by many of those in His day, and to this day still, as they expected a warrior king in glory to come…not an emptied carpenter who flipped the world upside down with radical humility and holiness. Christ did not renounce nor diminish His deity, just temporarily released the need to outwardly claim it and express it. This emptying that we read about in Philippians 2, especially verse 7, is countercultural, captivating, and compelling.

What might you be known for or have because of your position or title that you could serve out of or release for their gain and not for your own?

"TAKING THE FORM OF A SERVANT, BEING BORN IN THE LIKENESS OF MEN"

There are brilliant theologians and commentators who can unpack kenotic theory for you and dissect Greek for days. I am not one of those. I know enough to know that I have limits, aches and pains, and concerns that I understand God does not. God is all powerful, ever present, full of infinite wisdom. I am not. I have limits and faults. Jesus taking on humanity was quite a step toward us, creation, for the sake of our own saving. He did not do this and reign in a throne room on earth but came fragile and humble, first as a baby in a manger and then as a simple carpenter. Jesus' fragility, because of what He took on, is beautifully relatable to us.

The incarnation, remembered and celebrated by Christmas, is depicted beautifully in two of the Gospel accounts of Christ's birth, in Matthew and Luke. It is also more poetically described in John 1:14, especially the Message translation:

> *The Word became flesh and blood,*
> *and moved into the neighborhood.*
> *We saw the glory with our own eyes,*
> *the one-of-a-kind glory,*
> *like Father, like Son,*
> *Generous inside and out,*
> *true from start to finish.*

The beauty of the incarnation is exuding with humility. If the incarnation is the masterpiece, radical humility is the ethos. One cannot look at this piece of art, read this story, listen to its beautiful tune and not smell, taste, hear, and see humility. This is a profound and progressive step down into greater lowliness. He is God, but did not grasp at this, so He came as man...but not just as a man (like a rock star arriving to be worshipped) but as a bond-servant. And not just a servant but one that would...well, we will dive into that next.

How could you pursue servanthood, in humility, in the contexts and situations in which you would be expected to be served? What would that look like?

"BEING OBEDIENT TO THE POINT OF DEATH, EVEN DEATH ON THE CROSS."

One of the most confrontational and countercultural aspects of Jesus, especially in the context of interfaith dialogue, is the fact that He not only came to humbly serve but also to die for our sake. His death is confrontational to many. But we needed a sufficient sacrifice to atone for our sin, so Jesus had to empty Himself in radical humility. His obedience unto death is uncomfortable for many. It was brutal. The cross was a humiliating public death of a criminal. This is profoundly confrontational to our understanding and the world's.

This heroic humility is piercing. Sometimes we only see humility as quiet, meek, soft, gentle, releasing preference like a husband might do on date nights. "No babe, where do *you* want to eat?" This sort of humility we see in verse 8 and the crucifixion account throughout the Gospels is fierce, powerful, compelling, curse-breaking, and offensive. But it is pure sacrificial humility. Let us experience and pursue a more profound and all-encompassing humility, not just a corralled one that many of us know. This sort of humility is also needed, for the sake of the world. This humility has a perfect example—God came, putting on humanity's flesh, and served creation to the point of death, "even death on the cross." Jesus could do this because He knew who He was and, because of God's great love for us, was willing to empty Himself for our sake.

His humility is our hope. (Don't ruin this by thinking of Princess Leia.) The cross of Christ is a radical sign of humility. When we see it in our church, around someone's neck on jewelry, a part of someone's social media profile, or somewhere else, let us be reminded of Christ's radical and confrontational humility for our sake.

The picture of Jesus that we read about in Philippians 2 is captivating and is a compelling template for Christ-like humility. It's radical, sacrificial, and confident. This acts, in itself, as something that confronts our own pride and entitlement.

A CONFRONTATIONAL PRACTICE: PSALM 139

This intentional reading of Psalm 139 places me in the wide open, surrendered, for Him to probe and confront, revealing things and leading me to response. Multiple times a week, I read Psalm 139 to confront and respond. Sometimes this occurs before or after an intimidating meeting, sometimes after I feel extra tender from a relational connect, or in response to a poor mental day where I'm wrestling with something deeply. In the first twenty-two verses, I rest in the fact of being fully known, not being able to "run," and specific verses and words stick out and minister to me. I spend time reading these verses and thinking about them... possibly asking the simple questions of "What do I sense God highlighting or speaking to me?" and "What might I do about that?" After reading those twenty-two verses and responding, the actual contemplative work begins with four steps flowing out of verses 23 and 24. My responses to these prompts might be written down, possibly in a journal, typed into a simple notes page on my phone, or even shared openly with a friend or my wonderful wife. In verses 23 and 24, we are prompted to ask God to...

1. Search me and know my heart (our core being or heart).
2. Test me and know my anxious thoughts (our mind).
3. See if there is any offensive or harmful way in me (our actions, habits, manners).
4. Lead me in the way everlasting (submission to His guidance and leadership).

Every time I do this, He reveals and confronts something in my heart, an anxiety or thought that is destructive or at least distracting, and shines light on a habit that is not Christ-like or that is harmful. This is needed for us to regularly and rhythmically put us before the Lord's kind confrontations for our own formation. Once He reveals and confronts, I confess and submit to Him leading me in the everlasting way, *His way*.

Would you explore this practice in response to the content of this chapter, in honest interaction with Scripture, and an open heart to God? *This will require humility...*

———————

Lord, meet us and confront us. Heal the places where we have been wrongly confronted and naively formed by much lesser or broken things.

Jesus, we desire to look more like You by the time we finish reading this book so we relent and present ourselves fully, our pride included. Help those reading forget anything that is not helpful for their own formation and Kingdom impact...help them forget the words I've written...BUT if there is anything from You, thank You, and will it confront and find itself received by spiritually sensitive and hungry followers of Jesus.

Chapter 3

Crucible

"Lay me on an anvil, O God.
Beat me and hammer me into a crowbar.
Let me pry loose old walls.
Let me lift and loosen old foundations."

CARL SANDBURG, *PRAYERS OF STEEL*

Fire tests the purity of silver and gold,
but the LORD tests the heart.

PROVERBS 17:3, NLT

When my friend Dr. David Thomas looked at our small circle of leaders in the basement of Hughes and said, "You might want to consider keeping the chapel open through the night," I initially felt some hesitation about pressing forward. I had a sense that something was actually happening, but we had no clue that He was preparing our hearts to lead His people through the next sixteen days.

That basement meeting on the first night, consisting of a small group of leaders, became the first of many in which we were tested and refined as leaders and as followers of Jesus. As the sixteen days continued on, the storage closet behind the stage became a "boardroom" for the Outpouring core team. We dragged a whiteboard into this closet, leaned it up against a piano stand and boxes, and sat around and loosely mapped out the day approximately three or four hours at a time. We had rules, primarily putting our phones away and raising our hands before we could speak, that just formed as we went. It is a beautiful thing that the stewardship of this moment began in a closet. Thankfully, because of a growing team, we were able to move to a larger conference room.

During these meetings I felt like I received ten years of leadership development in sixteen days and at many times experienced the conviction and pressing of the Spirit on my ego, my leadership, and my own integrity. Like soldiers in a foxhole, those men and women I led beside in storage closets, stages, a conference room, and now around the world would become dear teammates in the work of God.

As people have asked about those days at Asbury, I've wanted to share about the refining gold in those meetings but it almost seems too tender and precious. Moments of weeping and moments of cheering interwoven with some of the most intense internal struggles and transformation I've experienced. The stakes felt so high and the desires of each individual in there to honor and steward these moments was so real. These meetings were a profound crucible to our individual souls and our leadership community. I experienced fast-paced reconciliation and restoration because of the holiness and necessity of the moment. I saw organizations topple over one another in service, humility, and kindness. There were moments of confession and courageous confrontation and correction. If ego and preference were being worked on in Hughes by the Spirit of God, those two very human realities were also in the crosshairs of God in the leadership meetings. Do you remember in elementary school when you might join hands with a couple friends and spin and spin and spin some more? The force on those sweet little fingers can become too much and you let go and fling every which way. It seemed like we, as stewards and facilitators of this deeply spiritual moment, found ourselves in the same posture, spinning and clinging, as we led this moment.

There is something so holy and so hopeful in these crucible moments. The cost is high but the potential is higher if we lean in and yield to the Spirit's refinement. When we find ourselves in these crucibles, the pressure and heat seemingly unbearable, they are the very places where we are formed and sanctified as leaders. These places will reveal sin, but even more, will cultivate the kind of repentance that leads to resilience and humility. We can steward these moments toward greater joy—a joy that is ultimately found in Jesus, who is quite familiar with the pain and pressure of the crucible.

A crucible, in its most practical sense, is a tool used to melt substances or at least submit a substance to very high temperatures. This tool, usually a container of some sort, can withstand the intensity in a way that the substance inside cannot. Gold and silver are purified through the use of a crucible and heat in which the heat is applied and the imperfections rise to the top to be taken away. In a less literal meaning, a crucible is a situation, trial, or season in which things collide, heat up, and interact in a manner that creates something new. I believe the crucible of discipleship, of the cross-shaped life, is the most consistent and widely shared experience for chasing humility in our lives. Like confrontation, the crucible heats up our being, revealing what needs to be scraped off and tossed, and we end up purer. Like compost, the difficulty is recycled for purpose, the purpose of our formation.

The crucible of that storage closet at Asbury was not my first and will not be my last. One of the most meaningful crucible moments happened on a similar college campus in a space very much like a storage closet…the laundry room.

DOING LAUNDRY WITH
BROTHER LAWRENCE

In a random hallway in the recreation center of Indiana Wesleyan University, there was a locked double door and just up and to the left of that door was a laundry chute. This hallway was just a couple steps away from a pretty nice basketball arena where the university's legacy basketball program played, and with a couple more steps and turns, there was the men's soccer team's locker room. I had played soccer since first grade but ultimately was never the best guy on the team, and once I got older and around more serious soccer players, it was clear that I was a much better encourager than goalkeeper. After reality set in, I looked at playing at a couple smaller schools but found myself with some really dear friends who were essential in introducing me to Jesus, and a soccer coach who had discipled me back in Colorado and now was coaching at this Christian university in the Midwest. The kicker is that this soccer team was much better than those I was talking to, so I was not utilized on the field, but instead served the men's soccer team in the work done through those double doors near the laundry chute. Most of my friends went there to play soccer and I was going to do their laundry.

I remember days that I would snag keys and load big laundry machines with my friends' practice gear, stinky socks, and sliders (a cooler way to say underwear). One time I could not get keys and was freaking out that the gear would not be ready for the next game or practice. That day, to get to my laundry job, I had to climb through the laundry chute (back then I was much more agile and slim...I could not imagine doing that now).

In the crucible of the laundry room, I first wrestled with a teammate calling me "servant." That word had never meant anything positive in my life. I had just met Jesus approximately two years prior. "You are such a servant" was not a compliment, ever, nor was it something I had set out to do when I dreamed of playing soccer in college. In a crucible of cleaning and folding laundry, I first listened to sermons and read books about Christ washing feet and His radical posture to those around Him. The dad of one of my close friends on the team gave me a copy of *Practicing the Presence of God* by Brother Lawrence and

I read it over and over in between cycles of washing and drying. Here are some of the quotes that I still have in my Bible today that I first read as a young believer cleaning sweaty undies...

"We ought not to be weary of doing little things for the love of God, who regards not the greatness of the work, but the love with which it is performed."

"God knoweth best what is needful for us, and all that He does is for our good. If we knew how much He loves us, we should always be ready to receive equally and with indifference from His Hand the sweet and the bitter: all would please that came from Him. The sorest afflictions never appear intolerable, except when we see them in the wrong light."

"Do not be discouraged by the resistance you will encounter from your human nature; you must go against your human inclinations. Often, in the beginning, you will think that you are wasting time, but you must go on, be determined and persevere in it until death, despite all the difficulties."

Brother Lawrence was my guide through a crucible of learning about obscurity, ordinariness, and the pursuit of humility. Like Brother Lawrence cooking in the kitchen of his monastery and meeting God in picking up straw (you should really read *Practicing the Presence of God*), I was being tested and shaped by God in folding soccer jerseys that I wished I was wearing, playing a game, and getting cheered for by loved ones in the stands. The truth I was hearing from Brother Lawrence,

Scripture, and in prayer mixed with my ego, the laundry, and my frustration. Like a chemical reaction, those things mixed and the heat was being turned up in my soul…like a crucible revealing all my pride, ego, and more. The work I needed to do, my emotional struggle doing it, plus the Spirit's power and encounter allowed those moments to be a surgery room for the Great Physician to diagnose and attack pride and entitlement.

I would have liked to say one of the greatest crucibles of character and purifiers of my ego was an epic theology class or the galvanizing comradery among teammates, but I can't. To this day, the crucible of the laundry room is a cherished season of deep formation in my life. Did an angel appear in between the washer and dryer upon the piles of sweaty clothes? No. Did the audible voice of God whisper "Well done, my good and faithful laundry boy"? No. Did Shekinah Glory fall in the racks of plastic hangers? I am unsure…probably not. But through the testing and difficulty of this opportunity, though I picked it and got very minimally paid for it, I became acquainted with the beautiful formation that can be experienced in a crucible. Over time, the laundry room became a sanctuary, even though it reeked of bleach, college dude musk, and Tide.

TEMPERING HUMILITY

A crucible is utilized in the activity of purifying and tempering metals. Tempering is simply the strengthening or improvement of a metal by heating it up and applying stress to it through hammering, cooling, and doing it all over again. The crucible is utilized to apply a high amount of heat to draw out the yuck of the substance, to be scraped off and thrown away, or to apply high stress to strengthen the substance. Both images, purifying and tempering, are powerful pictures to how circumstances, either every day following Jesus or difficult and trying moments of decisiveness, difficulty, and testing, can make us look more like Jesus. Tod Bolsinger, in his book *Tempered Resilience*, speaks of this sort of formation by inviting us to pursue the tempering of the crucible in our own discipleship journey. We must walk through the cross-shaped door to live a cruciform life. Both of those things rely on and lead to radical humility in Christ Jesus. This sort of humility keeps us in the crucible because we know He is God, He is doing the work, and we are submitted to His will in our own formation and His mission.

The heating of the crucible can come in a multitude of ways. Added stress, conflict and confusion, and just the difficulty of a situation applies formational heat to develop in us the resilient and powerful character of Christ. The working is that of every-day discipleship with Jesus. Ultimately, I am deeply convinced that everything can be a crucible.

ULTIMATELY, EVERYTHING'S FORMATIONAL

As we approach everything as a formational opportunity, whether it's an intimidating new season or just a frustrating morning where you spill your coffee, we must root our identity in Jesus for the hard work to be bearable. The rooted identity of a disciple in their adoption, secured salvation, and the uncon-ditional love of God will be tested in crucible moments. This is why in the "working," we are rooting ourselves into the core identities of being a beloved follower of Jesus. As the heating occurs or the hammering ensues, we must be rooted. *Humility is deep rootedness in who you are and who He is.*

When utilizing the imagery of the crucible, the heating is really where the work is happening in the most profound ways. It's working through confrontation with a coworker whom you disagreed with, humbly apologizing for being sharp or harsh while getting the kids ready for school or church, or circling back and clarifying a hurtful text or email. The key is identifying where the heat was applied and noticing that something icky appeared.

Blacksmiths, in the imagery of tempering, use forges. These are essential because there needs to be a safe, reliable, and almost predictable place and way for such heat and transformation to be applied. The substance is so vulnerable and is so tested, the blacksmith needs a space like the forge or crucible for this heating work to be done. In our lives, this really must be the same... the secret place with the Lord. The heating of self-reflection and growing awareness prepares you for tremendous working out of a strengthened self. Some questions I often ask myself in moments of self-reflection, or "heating," are:

- Are you handling your brokenness like Jesus would? Why or why not?
- Who are you becoming (forming) because of this situation and/or your response?

I ask these questions after meetings and Zoom calls, after finishing preaching, usually most effective for my formation, when I am parenting through a difficult situation. Jonathan Sacks contrasts the heroism of this sort of formation between the Greek and Jewish heroes: "The battles the Greek heroes had to fight were against their enemies. The battles their Jewish counterparts had to fight were against themselves: their fears, their hesitations, their sense of unworthiness." This is that second kind of battle…and it is worth it.

This battle doesn't always need to, or should not, stay between you and the Lord. It can be an intimate and intentional conversation with a small group or in your private time with the Lord. I personally have experienced this occurring in both of those contexts or with meaningful time with my sweet Kristin or my counselor. In the experience of the tempering work of forming humility is the necessity of relying on relationships, "thick and heavy relationships,"[1] as Bolsinger explains. Three sort of relationships that I have in my life that aid in the formational work of "holding" can be explained through men in the Bible and their role in the story of God. The teammates you should pursue and gather are:

Jethro—Exodus 18

Jethro was a Midianite priest and the father-in-law to Moses, one of the most impactful men in biblical history. During the crucible moment of Moses' journey, he had to pick humility and allow his father-in-law to coach and encourage him. Moses bumped up against his own limits and within those limits began to feel the crucible of leadership and formation. Jethro mentored and coached Moses through this and offered a "pressure release valve" while still dignifying and supporting his son-in-law's own calling and abilities. We need a Jethro, a coach or mentor, to offer little pressure valves when we are experiencing the humbling work in the crucible. Some questions that could help discern a Jethro in your journey to chase humility…

- Whom do you feel safe enough to give permission to engage you and submit to when they coach and mentor you in the crucible?
- Who has gone through a crucible and come out on the other side as a disciple that you'd like to resemble?

Barnabas—Acts 4, 9, 11, 15

In one of Paul's first crucibles, we meet a man called Barnabas, which means "son of encouragement." As we are experiencing the heating up of the crucible in our own journey toward greater humility, we just sometimes need someone to see us and encourage us. Barnabas did just this for Paul through identifying Paul, vouching for Paul in the midst of Christian community, and walking with Paul for a season of formation. This required Paul's humility to accept the encouragement and care of his peer Barnabas, while revealing the reality that we all need a spiritual cheerleader once in a while. Some questions for you as you identify your Barnabas, a peer, in your journey of chasing humility...

- Whom do you humbly listen to when they speak truth, not just compliments, into your life?
- Whom in your life do you trust to see and hear what they describe so that you really receive their words?

The Armor Bearer—1 Samuel 14

The armor bearer is a nameless man who was right alongside Jonathan, the son of King Saul, at a key moment of his own journey. We do not know much about this armor bearer besides what history tells us about this role and the words of this passage, and you know who is okay with that? The armor bearer. That is what he signed up for. In his heroism, he did not need to be named, but just served Jonathan. In verse 7, after Jonathan proposes a bold act, the armor bearer says, "Do all that you have in mind…Go ahead; I am with you heart and soul" (NIV). Who in your journey does not need to be named but champions you and your journey like this young armor bearer? The crucible is hard and the process might lead to some courageous and humbling steps, but an armor bearer can sit in that meeting, read over that text or email or whatever you need as you take your courageous step…all without praise or shout-outs because he or she is with you, heart and soul.

Here are some questions for you as you discern who might serve you on your journey of pursuing greater Christ-like humility…

- Whom do you feel safe with to share your courageous steps with and allow them to walk with you in authentic vulnerability?
- Who in your life does not need nor want anything from you but just to see you succeed?

The humbling work in the crucible is hard. As this hard work occurs, community can carry us and keep us in that sweet spot where deep formation occurs. The tempering continues with the imagery of hammering, cutting and shaping, and then plunging the hot metal into cool water…shocking it. This specific moment, shocking the heated and hammered metal, helps the tool or metal get even stronger. This is important work, which represents the difficulty of being in those crucible moments as they form humility in us and after, we rest. These are rhythms of exertion and rest, like the restful practices of silence and sabbath that follow the hard tempering work of formation or mission. Remember, the difference is not going to come from hustling but from humbling yourself. Abide in Jesus in the crucible, and the Spirit will do the transforming work with you.

One of *my* most formational crucible moments, that tested all my abiding endurance, was at a doughnut shop.

THE CRUCIBLE OF MAKING DOUGHNUTS

During my first years of vocational ministry, there was a local doughnut shop that acted as my office most days. During this season of ministry, our church experienced a traumatic season of multiple leaders having significant failures that led to them being let go. This was the beginning of a crucible season, the heating up of my spiritual journey. In the midst of this trying season, while also struggling to bear the weight of growing responsibilities, I came face-to-face with my own brokenness.

I had struggled and was still struggling in a season of brokenness. I found myself speaking words and stories that were half-truths, enhanced narratives, or even just downright lies. As I was overwhelmed, intimidated, and insecure…I found myself caught in my brokenness and out of pride I didn't ask for help but covered up and hid behind the stories and lies. This led to my personal failure of character and stepping down from being on staff. *I write these words, even now, with sobriety and an immense amount of gratitude for the freedom, work, and ultimately the Gospel-given identity I sit in and write from today.* The beauty of these moments was that, even though I thought I was a goner, done for good, and too broken, Jesus was ready (as was my praying wife) with hope and vision for healing and freedom. I resigned and entered a generous restoration process with my denomination and began to start working at my previous "second office," the local doughnut shop.

After working at a beautiful but messy church, doing what I felt was pretty impressive for a kid like me, I was now waking up at 3:30 in the morning to make doughnuts and lattes for guests. My wife held me in the humbling heat of the crucible, reminding me of who I am and the worth of staying in the crucible. A mentor, Ed, coached me and included me on ministry trips to remind me of the worth of the work and that I was not done. The doughnut shop manager, a pastor with a similar story, did not get any praise or a raise for what he did for me but cheered me on and allowed me to go to every counseling appointment or class I was assigned to go to. Many friends cheered me on and encouraged me, like Barnabas, to do the work in the crucible of doughnuts, lattes, counseling, and hard conversations. *The crucible of healing and humility, while covered in flour and coffee grounds, was working.*

One morning, some of my past teammates on staff came to the doughnut shop for a meeting. This was not humbling but humiliating…I wanted to hide.

The crucible experience narrated by self, others,
or Satan is humiliating, but the humbling you experience in
*the crucible is **the Holy Spirit and Jesus' kindness in forming you.***
If Christ is inviting you lower, then there is life and provision
there for you. If you oblige the enemy's invitation to
humiliation, there is no sustaining provision or protection
there. Christ is not in the business of humiliating us.
Who are you letting narrate your crucible moments?

Not only did I want to hide...I wanted to run. Christ was inviting me to go lower, but when my boss at the shop asked me to jump out from behind the bar and clean tables and windows, I was confronted by my pride.

"Are you kidding me?" I whispered to myself as tears began to well up in my eyes.

"Can I wait for a little while, please?" I asked my boss, to hopefully give me time until my old teammates finished and left.

"*Are you freaking kidding me, Jesus, please get me out of here.*" I prayed in frustration and anger.

"No. I really need you to do this now, Zach. Thanks," said my boss.

I grabbed a rag and spray bottle and walked outside. The doughnut shop had two full walls of windows and my team was having a meeting at its farthest window. I would start cleaning, extra slow...I mean meticulously, to make sure I had ample time for the team's meeting to end and for them to leave. I did the first window and dreamed of getting in my car and leaving. I did the second window and tears were running down my cheeks...the lies of the enemy whispering humiliating predictions of my future and my worth. I did the third window... close to rounding the corner to that last window by the staff meeting. I started to pray. "Lord, please help me do this." I had a couple more windows to go as I rounded the corner.

As I rounded the corner for the final stretch, I started feeling joy. I began to imagine Jesus cleaning His disciples' feet and then...cleaning the window with me. The Holy Spirit began forming me with His kindness.

If the King of Kings would clean doughnut shop windows with me, what did I have to be embarrassed about?

What was my pride lying to me about?

What was my ego whispering to me in those moments?

I felt Jesus with me as I came to the final window, with my old staff sitting right on the other side of the glass, talking to me about my identity and His love for me. Before spraying the glass and wiping it down…I pressed my face up against the glass and blew a big raspberry. I cleaned that window with joy and gratitude that in the matter of just a few windows, Jesus had transformed a humiliating moment into a meaningful, humbling crucible. And guess what I did next?

Put in my two weeks' notice.

Finished my restoration process.

And began to plant a beautiful church.

Are you in a personal crucible season that seems to just be humiliating? Do you feel alone, with no Jethros, Barnabases, or armor bearers in the crucible? How might you invite Jesus to narrate the crucible instead of yourself…changing the story from humiliation and frustration to humility and freedom?

Thank God for doughnut shops with Jesus. I would not be writing this book and telling these stories if it were not for my Jethro, Barnabas, and armor bearer/general manager holding me in the crucible of heating and healing.

THE CRUCIBLE OF BEARS & LIONS
AND HIDING IN CAVES

There was a young Hebrew man, the youngest of many brothers, who would make a home in the obscure places of Bethlehem while tending to his father's sheep. This young man would experience the hard and lonely work of a shepherd as his father,

Jesse, did his work at home. When the prophet Samuel arrived in the city, Jesse favored the older sons and practically wrote off his youngest in the field, minding the sheep. In the gritty work of shepherding the sheep, something was being formed in this young man, David. David had fought off lions and bears that tried to snag his father's sheep. David had fallen in love with God and somehow, in the hiddenness of the crucible, became prepared to be anointed and step forward as the next king of Israel. David was not just "minding the sheep" but was being prepared in the crucible of shepherding, fighting off lions and bears, and, I imagine, meeting with and getting to know the Lord in intimate ways. Intimate enough ways that when a giant named Goliath started talking trash about his God, he would not stand for it.

So many times, when I read the story of David and Goliath, found in 1 Samuel 17, I think of how I would walk out this story. David had been formed in ways that would be expressed beautifully in this collision with Goliath. David knew who he was and who he was not and stood firm in his identity when he denied the king's armor that did not fit. This consecrated confidence confronts people-pleasing and self-protection. David did not deny the armor to make a point or flex his courage. He did it because it simply did not fit. He knew who he was and what he could do without armor . . . He did not have it when the lions and bear came to kill his father's sheep.

How many times do I do something epic or dramatic, like deny someone else's "armor" or way of doing things, not out of security and identity, but to flex, make a point, or be impressive?

David was not trying to impress the king, his brothers, or the flanks of soldiers shuddering at Goliath's verbal abuse. David, in the crucible of shepherding, had fallen in love with the Lord and knew God's worth. David took a stand and faced Goliath with consecrated confidence because Goliath was defying God's army…Goliath was attacking the God David had met and lived for in private. God had kept David and been with him in private and David, in public, was not going to stand for his God and God's army to be attacked. I imagine David saying under his breath, "No one talks that way about my God."

How many times might I do something with mixed motives, some for self and some in "Jesus' name," with an eye on the task and an eye on the audience?

David locked eyes with Goliath, with no armor and no desire to impress, and ran toward the giant. With consecrated confidence, holy humility, David told the Philistine:

"You come against me with sword and spear and javelin, but I come against you in the name of the LORD Almighty, the God of the armies of Israel, whom you have defied" (v. 45).

David would kill Goliath and walk into new favor and anointing for the remainder of his life. The crucible of shepherding and fighting lions and bears would soon become the crucible of hiding from the king who once offered him armor. Saul, out of jealousy and fear, would come against David and hunt to kill the young man who would soon take his seat as king. David would evade the angry king and fight the urge to retaliate. The crucible of formation in David's life had continued from the obscure season of shepherding to a more intense and difficult season of running and hiding.

One of the most powerful segments of David's story, and I believe an important crucible moment of the future king, is found in 1 Samuel 24. David's crucible is described in verses 4–7. The heart of David and his sensitivity to the Spirit are sweetly spoken in verse 6, *"The LORD forbid that I should do such a thing to my master, the LORD's anointed, or lay my hand on him; for he is the anointed of the LORD."*

The crucible of David's life had produced holy humility and that character confronted Saul powerfully. David's desire was not for relief but to be a man after God's own heart. <u>*When we are in the crucible, might our goal be to exit the crucible more like Christ and not just relieved from the discomfort.*</u> David would continue in the crucible though and continue to be formed by God as he experienced the heat. David would soon become king and even when he failed, he was known as a man after God's own heart. Humble...flawed...but humble.

THE CRUCIBLE OF THE DESERT AND TEMPTATION

Though Christ did not need the crucible moment to form radical humility, purity, and courage in Him, we see a crucible season of forty days that offers to us some suggestions for standing strong in these moments and coming out not only intact but deeply formed (Luke 4:1–14, Matthew 4:1–11, and Mark 1:11–13). Jesus went through these forty days fasting and praying, while facing great temptations from Satan. So how do we walk in a crucible moment like Jesus? We do it by being:

- **Filled with the Spirit**—We are invited to experience the fresh filling of the Holy Spirit as we walk through life. The crucible of formation is unbearable and will be wasted without the Spirit's power. Without the Spirit, the crucible leaves us quite hopeless and reliant on our own strength, competency, capacity, and knowledge. Even if we are impressive, strong, capable, and brilliant, we will miss out and even suffer these moments without the Spirit's power and presence.

I have walked into seasons filled with confidence and competency that have not led to formation. I have experienced a crucible moment filled with human courage and strength along with vision and strategy, but it led to disappointment, greater suffering, and I don't know if I looked much more like Jesus and less like Zach after the experience.

- **Led by the Spirit**—I am afraid many of us find ourselves in crucible moments because we have wandered into them, following our own will and ideas instead of the Spirit. A crucible initiated by the Spirit has tremendous potential. When I force it, initiating it for my gain, relief, or breakthrough, I often experience difficulty as compared to when I relent and allow the Spirit to initiate the work the way it desires. When I grind and hustle formation outside of the Spirit's guidance and power, there is greater pain and even shrapnel that impacts others. Instead of crucible moments spurred on by me, possibly even from my own disobedience and wandering, I would rather the Spirit initiate and lead. When the Spirit leads us, we can walk in greater confidence and hope for the formation that awaits us. When the Spirit leads us into the crucible, we can walk with some spiritual swagger of expectation and hope. With consecrated confidence, we can grow tremendously and leave the crucible looking a bit more like Christ.

- **Rooted and confident in Scripture**—Jesus combatted Satan's invitations and lies with truth from Scripture. When temptations come your way, what do you fight them with? Your own might? Your own comeback saturated with some spiritualized sassiness? I sadly do this often, but as soon as I cling to and declare the Word of God, I am reminded of its power. Jesus did not white-knuckle and grit His teeth to win the battle, but rested in the power of Scripture. How might you and I grow in our knowledge and reliance on the Word so in crucible seasons and out of crucible season, we can stand on the solid rock of God's Word? We wouldn't be shaken or intimidated but clear and confident, humbly reliant on Scripture.

- **Knowing who we are**—I smirk at how Satan shows his cards so recklessly that I would have to be blind to miss it. While reading about Jesus' temptation in the desert, I smirk at Satan's words to Jesus in those crucible moments. Satan saying, "If you are the son of God…" is like me looking at my wife, while wearing a ring and having a home full of wedding photos and saying, "If you are my wife…" Of course sweet KP is my bride! Jesus' authority and strength rest in this fact that He knew and knows exactly who He is. Satan was once an angel who would have been worshipping the Son in heaven before Satan retaliated and was banished. When Satan commands Jesus to worship him for the sake of authority and glory, it is like me stopping someone in traffic, asking them to roll down the window, and offering them a candy bar for their beautiful new car that they own already. First, the candy is so small in comparison to what they are actually experiencing, enjoying, and owning, and second, they do not need to give me their car…it is *theirs*. Satan is helpless, like he was with Jesus in the wilderness, when we just know who we are.

- **Knowing our end goal**—Though Jesus was just getting started, we know that He was sent out of love for the fallen world to redeem and reconcile all of creation back to Himself. When we read John 3:16, in Scripture or on Tim Tebow's eye black, we see Jesus fasting and praying while being tempted by Satan. Jesus knew exactly where this was all going to end. Not only does Jesus, in His all-knowing and all-powerful Self, know that the cross and resurrection is set before Him to give us freedom and reconciled relationship but He also knows how the entire story ends like we read in Revelation. In the same way, in much less mysterious, spiritual, and eschatological ways, when we are in the midst of the crucible, we can gain strength and perseverance as we experience the heating and hammering when we set our eyes on the outcome of deep formation into Christ-like humility. Like a hard workout, a difficult class in school, or a deeply trying season of counseling, we can be held in the heat of formation with a vision and commitment to where this is headed without hopelessness. We might not know where it exactly ends, like a job or a certain geography, but if we place our feet and set our eyes on looking more like Jesus by the end of our crucible, I believe we can endure quite a bit.

A PRACTICE FOR THE CRUCIBLE

The crucible, ripe in formational potential, is inevitable for the Christian and should be soberly expected with hope and sensitivity. Rich Villodas, a pastor and author on formation and culture, speaks about how our responses to things are invaluable revelations to a deeper thing in us, good or bad, that can be explored. This is essentially the heating of the crucible. Villodas offers some wonderful self-reflection questions that I have saved on my phone and use often.

- What happened that caused the response?
- What do I feel now?
- What story am I telling myself?
- What does the Gospel story say about that?
- What non-instinctual response do I need to take?

With a focus on chasing humility, this set of questions can help reveal, heat up, hammer, and hew us in our crucible.

———————

Lord, will You walk us into crucible moments with evident presence and supernatural peace and will anything written by me that does not honor You nor lead to Spirit-empowered fruit in the reader's life be forgotten and be tossed aside but if any of this content might be inspired by You meaningfully from Your Word, for the sake of the reader's formation and pursuit of greater humility and healing, would You bless it and would it bear fruit in my brother or sister's life.

Thank You, Lord, for the doughnut shops and laundry rooms of our lives...give us endurance and renewed vision for their potential in our lives. Amen.

Chapter 4

Crushing

"If you are going to offer a complaint to God it
must be done with a humble heart...
Proud, demanding questions from a heart that
believes it is owed something from God will never
lean into true lament. Before you start complaining,
be sure you've checked your arrogance at the door.
Come with your pain, not your pride."

MARK VROEGOP,
DARK CLOUDS, DEEP MERCY

"Suffering is actually at the heart
of the Christian story."

TIMOTHY KELLER

Eden sat on the altar as I kneeled in front of it, her arms and legs wrapped around me and her head nuzzled into my neck. Her fiery red hair was all up in my business, but I did not care... Eden, Dad, and our Father were at the altar. These days were intense for her. Her dad was down at Asbury and she knew God was moving in a unique way. She came most days, Chick-fil-A or coloring books in hand, and worshipped, danced, and saw her sweet college-aged friends engage with God's Spirit. Eden wanted to go to the altar this evening with me. She sat and asked me to be quiet. I was quiet. She told me someone was yelling in her ear. I asked if the voice sounded nice or mean... Eden replied, "Oh, so nice but really loud."

"Okay... well, that might be Jesus, Eden. What is He saying?" I responded.

"'I love you, Eden, and I want you to [*a sweet and personal invite from the Lord for my daughter... that is hers to share someday*],'" Eden replied.

I cried and cried. A sweet woman, the wife of one of my seminary professors, scooted over and prayed over my daughter and me. It was one of my greatest treasures of the Outpouring.

College students from all over, weary and hopeful pastors, prayer warriors who had contended for this for ages, addicts, battered women, and curious onlookers would find themselves at the altar. Vape pens, smartphones, dime bags, and other things were collected, resulting from times of confession and relinquishing what had led them to that struggle. The blind receiving sight, dear ones stepping up and walking from wheelchairs, tumors disappearing, and many more supernatural encounters were witnessed and testified about. We are still hearing stories today as we travel and meet new people who joined us during those sixteen days. My friend David has said many times, "If we could see the altar with spiritual eyes, there would be piles and piles of broken chains covering it." This visual was only emphasized by the carpet under the altar being regularly saturated, wet with tears. It was and is a beautiful testimony of God's holy crushing.

The work God was doing in Hughes was, and still is, unforgettable. But to be honest, it was not always the easiest place for me to be. There was difficulty there; disappointments, questions raised, reminders of great loss, bubbling cynicism, exhaustion. The weight of the moment we were in was often felt most heavily for me there or outside, with the up to nine-hour lines and the warning for my family and me not to go outside without security. The weight of this began to feel really heavy. We had to be close to Jesus and even there, we felt the pressing and crushing of this moment. I know His yoke is easy and His burden is light (Matthew 11:28–30), but the significance of the moment was confronting and heating up areas of my life that I would just rather not deal with in front of fifty to sixty thousand folks. As God was moving in our midst, my fragile self had to cling to 2 Corinthians 4:7–10 as I led and mourned, as I facilitated and processed, and as I stewarded and lamented.

But we have this treasure in jars of clay to show that this all-surpassing power is from God and not from us. We are hard pressed on every side, but not crushed; perplexed, but not in despair; persecuted, but not abandoned; struck down, but not destroyed. We always carry around in our body the death of Jesus, so that the life of Jesus may also be revealed in our body.

As I got to encounter God with my family, I was keenly aware of someone missing. Esther Joy, my middle daughter, was watching this whole thing from heaven. As I prayed over other people's sick or hurting children, I also carried the disappointment of losing Esther Joy. As I met with a family whose child had just entered hospice, I remembered Esther Joy. As I met a sweet family that had driven thirty-plus hours to possibly get their daughter help, I prayed a wimpy prayer, feeling so overwhelmed and missing my sweet girl. I've told the story of that family and my "wobbly-knee prayer" often and the reality is that I do not know how their daughter is doing, nor any of the other children, marriages, ministries, and more that I prayed over. This is a weight that is heavy. This is a crushing and stirring that drives you down into Jesus and His fullness and healing. This is the humbling work as whole and embodied people. When we allow ourselves to be fully ourselves, not compartmentalizing areas of our lives like parenting, marriage, or ministry, but stand up as whole beings... the Spirit uses us and forms us through His weighty presence and power.

WHERE ELSE WOULD I GO?

Approximately two and a half years prior to the Asbury Outpouring, in the midst of the Covid pandemic, my wife and I found out that we were pregnant. We could not have been more excited. We loved life with our sweet Eden Mae, who was three years old at the time, but were excited about our new addition. We went to our first appointment, masks on our faces and checking in at the hospital doors. We got ushered back to the sonogram room and the nurse started to search for our baby. I heard the heartbeat quickly after and my sweet KP and I squeezed each other's hands.

A month later, we got to go in for our next sonogram. We would find out the gender and we already had a name picked out for a boy and a girl. When we learned it was a girl, we knew she was Esther Joy Meerkreebs. After the sonographer finished, she stepped out of the room. Shortly after, we heard a knock on the door and in walked a doctor. This doctor, who is now a dear friend, began to talk in a calm, gentle voice and slowly explained the terrible news that our daughter had a severe brain abnormality. She would most likely pass in utero, he said. If she did make it to birth, there was still a very small chance that we would not have much more than a few hours to a couple days with sweet Esther Joy.

I remember rocking my head against the cinderblock wall, gritting my teeth, tears streaming down my face. I was squeezing my wife's hand in our rhythmic squeeze-squeeze-squeeze, which was our makeshift way to say "I-LOVE-YOU" when words just don't work. No competency or special skill I might have or knowledge I might acquire could serve us here. Nothing that I could have flexed or put on a résumé could have helped us in that appointment. All of my gifting, experiences, degrees, woo, and charisma had nothing on this diagnosis. Humbling. This began our heaviest crushing yet...the most difficult season I have ever walked through.

We were told that we did not need to come back if we did not want to, but of course we did...every week, to hear her sweet heart beat not knowing what would happen next. We were going to parent Esther Joy as long as we could. We became friends with sonographers and our high-risk OB-GYN physician. We leaned into the crushing of this season as committed parents to Esther Joy. Both of our work families championed our journey and created space for us to go to every appointment and partner well in parenting. We would meet with Esther's palliative care team soon. They said lots of things I did not understand (KP was the medical one; I just studied the Bible) but when I did understand, I knew it was all bad news. We would need to start making decisions that began to get scarier and scarier and all more real. Within months, we were told there were some concerns about my sweet KP's health as well, which made birthing plans more complicated, and I was absolutely terrified. My spiritual journey was flayed open to Jesus and those I was journeying with. Absolutely honest, messy, angry, confused, and laser focused on my wife and my littlest girl.

On Saturday morning, December 5, sweet KP woke me up and told me that her water had broken. This was six weeks earlier than we had planned with palliative care—and our OB-GYN in hopes of delivering the healthiest little girl we could. We headed to the hospital with a level of sobriety I've never felt before. By the next morning Esther Joy had arrived, surprising our doctors with more strength than expected, with curly brown hair and a little fold on her ear like mine. Sweet KP was healthy and there were no complications or concerns. It was an incredibly special and sober day, with Esther meeting her big sister, grandparents, and many friends over FaceTime, along with watching a soccer game with her dad. This day lasted exactly twelve hours and twelve minutes, and then Esther Joy went to be with the Lord. The crushing was so real that even my physical body had to express it and I had a stinking bloody nose for hours! All I could say was "Jesus, have mercy on Esther" as I introduced my little girl to Jesus and prayed. Crushed.

The next week was a heartbreaking blur that culminated in a celebration of Esther Joy's life. Our community was heroic, planning the service, providing meals, wanting to give resources for headstones and cemetery plots, and more. We had rides to every appointment and a spiritual big brother or mentor to walk us through the meetings. Beloved friends spoke, led prayer, played music, and my dear accountability partner, Esther's uncle Andy, preached one of the best sermons I had ever heard. Eden Mae interrupted another friend's song with her ukulele and insisted on a rendition of "Old MacDonald Had a Farm." The church rang out with oinks and moos to honor Esther Joy's beloved older sister. That day I preached from the end of John 6 and shared how the crushing had brought us to a humble realization of Peter's posture. Jesus asks the hard question to His twelve apostles after miracles, teaching, and many disciples leaving. I had to answer it too. You have to. We have to. In the crushing, Jesus asks, "You do not want to go away also, do you?" (John 6:67, NASB). I had always imagined the next part, Peter's confession, as Captain America or Iron Man from *The Avengers* when everyone comes back through those twinkling circles. But these days, in the crushing, I heard Peter's confession differently. I heard quaking in his voice, knowing what he had given up and who he had seen leave... trembling sobriety and a deep relinquishment to Jesus...

"Lord, where else would I go?"

Or in the Message according to Zach, "Jesus, are you kidding me? Where else would I run?"

And with a more settled voice, possibly with a gulp or crack, "*You* have the words of eternal life. We have believed and now have come to know that *You* are the Holy one of God."

I shared this at my daughter's funeral, voice cracking and snot running, in the midst of the crushing. I clung to it on that day, I clung to it at Asbury, and I cling to it now, in the midst of crushing, as I write this chapter (with tears and snot flowing) and invite you not to waste the crushing in our journey toward holy and set apart humility. Have you believed that He is who He says He is? Have you come to know that He is the Holy one of God even in the crushing and pressing? *Where else would you go?*

NEW WINE, NEW OIL

On the eighth day of the sixteen weighty and beautiful days at Asbury, I had hit my limit. The fullness of the day mixed with the weight of calling for this moment collided with two specifically difficult moments, one with a troubled young man in the parking lot and later that day with a heartbroken family longing for healing for their daughter, their daughter with the same brain abnormality as my Esther Joy. I prayed a wobbly-knee prayer for that family, about half "Lord come in power and heal this little one. Do the thing we so longed for for this sweet family" and half "Dear God, get me out of here!" I was weak, exhausted, and felt so fragile.

After the long day, I got in my car and started the twenty-minute drive home from Wilmore to Lexington. I could not wait to climb in bed with my wife and decompress. I cried and cried on that drive and texted two men who were carrying a similar weight stewarding these moments, Dr. Brown and Dr. Thomas. They both, compassionate and wise, encouraged me to get some sleep, not set an alarm, and reach out again in the morning. The next day, I came downstairs and talked to and prayed with my bride, sweet KP. She, like the prophet and partner she is, told me that I needed to get in my car and head back to be a part of what God was doing and talk to Him on the way about how I was feeling. She made me a smoothie, a cup of coffee, and I got in the car.

As I was driving and praying, I began to cry. I felt a pressing and crushing I had not felt before. Overwhelmed, intimidated, burdened, and fierce for those who had come from all over the world at this point, I began to pray to God and ask, "How will I do this? It feels way too heavy, Lord!"

"This will not crush you because I have already crushed you, son."

"Crushed me...I know...I can't bear it."

"I crushed you in private so you can serve new wine in public."

I wept...I knew what He was talking about. The tears, questions, screaming, more tears, snot. The silence. Some striving to be spiritual, which led to exhaustion, then more tears. In my blue chair, in the prayer closet, with my counselor, with my friends, and with my bride, I had been crushed by the loss of my daughter piled upon other seasons of great difficulty and trauma from the first thirty-two years of my life. *Can you relate?* Have you felt the weight and the pressing? Have you felt crushed?

I responded to God in a raw prayer: "Nope, not good enough. How will I do this?"

"I have pressed you in private. You have new anointing oil for the public."

I do not hear God like this often. I have wiggled around theological differences, denominations, and had differing deep experiences in my faith from the mission field, church plants, large established churches, Bible schools, and prayer rooms. God had generously met me in my Honda Pilot for such a time as this, narrating the season I was in and clarifying the out-coming of the crushing. As He dignified the crushing pain of loss and disappointment, he also designated me for a moment. It was the crushing and commissioning all in one. That's some-times how it works, huh? *Crushing and commissioning can go hand in hand.*

Have you ever sensed this? Dignifying your pain and desig-nating your purpose? The humbling work of suffering well, the crushing, can provide new wine and new oil for your season. Possibly not even just for a season, because clarifying your call-ing and anointing you for that work, the crushing and pressing, might clarify your purpose. There is a new message and deep-ened convictions that I carry because of my crushing. I will not lead, preach, and care the same way. The crushing is meant to do two things: get out of you what's in you and get the true you out of the thin skin that encases you. The crushing of the grape not only expresses the juice from the flesh, but it also separates the unusable parts of the grape from the juice.

The crushing and all it requires is a powerful tool to humble a man or woman. The crushing, stewarded well in partnership between you and the Spirit, will not be wasted and it will pro-duce new wine in your life and for those you love and care for. We so wish this was through a certification, a degree, or a tool belt you have, but often it's the humbling work of crushing that provides what's next for you. In the crushing, your identity and calling are crystallized along with your priorities and convic-tions for how you move ahead. The humbling work of remov-ing the old and unneeded through the pain and loss you've experienced keeps you low and dependent on the Father.

There is something significant to the holiness and intimacy of the crushing. Only now, and only in a few ways, do people know about the crushing reality that has taken sweet KP and me lower. That work, the work of crushing and pressing, is carefully stewarded by the Spirit in those moments and spaces that are hidden away and obscure.

Like the wine press...

Like the olive press...

Like the barrel set aside in obscurity to ferment...

Like the prayer closet or blue chair in your living room...

Like your counseling appointment or morning date to connect with your spouse.

From the private pressing comes the new oil of anointing to serve new wine. This takes new wineskins, right? You don't put new wine in old wineskins, so there is a new way to steward the crushing for you. In context, we know that through the further fermentation of the new wine, the old wineskins would burst with the fresh wine...ruining the new work. Old wine, still good, is in the old wineskin while the new wineskin, as it continues to be worked out, needs the pliability and flexibility of the new. Our new wineskin might just need that pliability, flexibility, and freshness to steward the continued work to keep it from bursting.

As we journey lower in humility, there might be new wineskins we need to embrace.

NEW WINESKINS

God is continually doing a new thing. He is in the business of renewal and with that comes new ways of doing things. In

Luke 5, Jesus speaks about the reality of new wine and new wineskins: "*No one pours new wine into old wineskins. Otherwise, the new wine will burst the skins; the wine will run out and the wineskins will be ruined. No, new wine must be poured into new wineskins.*" This does not mean to throw out all old wineskins, as many people think, but to paint a picture of stewarding a new thing, the new wine, in the pliable and capable wineskin. New wine in you, through crushing, needs to be stewarded in humility and new wineskins. Many people miss out on the new wine because they stay rigid and stubborn, especially in moments of pain and suffering.

Humility can thrive when suffering is stewarded well. Pride is inevitable when suffering is allowed to wreak havoc and do what it will. You probably have seen this, sadly, much more than suffering stewarded well, as suffering can so quickly, and so unhindered, lead to selfishness, bitterness, and pride. Suffering whispers to retreat and self-protect, to fight for what we are entitled to, and to make a point. What if suffering can both strengthen our agency (in a God-honoring way) and also lead us to a lower place of humility? The interior work of the crushing and pressing, stewarded by Jesus in us through practices and vulnerability, can do just that. I know both the difficulty of suffering well and also the potential coming from pain. There were seasons when suffering well could have been defined as "living well" in the world's eyes, with lots of DoorDash, Netflix, and naps. I do believe that in our suffering we need to be kind to ourselves, and in trauma and pain I have learned well to fight for fun and not to "should on yourself." But in a conversation of formation, in the pursuit of a captivating humility for a world full of pride and an "I'm gonna get mine" attitude, might we ask the question of how to let our suffering, the crushing, be a tool for our own formation and His mission!

In suffering, there are multiple things that might be "new wineskins" for you to both experience the new wine and grow in lowliness.

HONESTY

One thing that helps someone feeling the weight of disappointment, pain, and loss is clinging to something that seemingly is a dear friend to humility: *honesty*. Honesty allows us to be real with the gap in our life and leads to vulnerable naming where we have been wrong or even left in the dark, disagreeing, or just dumbfounded about how and why this occurred.

Honesty holds the door for humility to come in.

What is funny about this is that Christians stink at honesty. I am not saying that all my Christian brothers and sisters are liars and lack integrity, but I do think we are often not great at being brutally honest with where we are and how we feel.

Raw...authentic...vulnerable...known.

The Church can feel like a spiritual locker room, our Bible studies or small groups can be soaked in competition and comparison, and many of us have not learned that total honesty, being known, is some of the secret sauce of stewarding life as Christ followers. Jesus is a gentleman and will not yank you around or bust in on you (at least most of the time), but waits for you to come to the end of yourself in honesty. Honesty can make you feel very vulnerable and almost naked...totally seen for what you are, what you're asking, struggling with, and more. Dishonesty does this. As God wants to be in our disappointment and failure with us, we often hide out of shame or guilt. Honesty combats hiding and puts us out there to be addressed and cared for by God, and often those He has sent to walk with us.

Strahan Coleman wrote a beautiful prayer that highlights and equips us to lean into this sort of honesty: *"Unpeel me, Father, and bare my inner world, that in being who I really am, I may see who you really are."*[1]

As you are going through the crushing and pressing, how are you doing at being honest? Really honest with the questions you are asking, the pain you are feeling, the shame you are sitting in, or something else. Our honesty keeps our full self on the potter's wheel for the potter (Jeremiah 18) to continue to mold us. Our dishonesty hides us away from the potential formation and freedom that is offered. There are many ways to step into deeper honesty in your crushing, but here are some ideas:

- Join a "band" or accountability group with safe friends.
- Begin to journal.
- Utilize creativity to be really honest and raw—painting, poetry, songwriting, sketching.
- Embrace the practice of confession, being raw and honest with God.
- Explore a daily examen prayer so that you can identify and name the places of pain and disappointment in your life.

FRAGILITY

We are creatures, created beings, and God has not come to cancel that reality and make us superheroes. Yes, we are filled with the Spirit of God and we are Spirit empowered for endurance, grit, patience, joy, and much more, *but*, at the end of the day, we are creatures and He is the Creator. This reality, our fragility, is spoken about in freeing passages all over the Word of God and this keeps us fully aware of our limits and deep need for Him. Here are a few passages that help remind me of my fragility.

- James 4:14 (NKJV)—"*You do not know what* will happen *tomorrow. For what is your life? It is even a vapor that appears for a little time and then vanishes away.*"
- Psalm 103:14–16 (TLB)—"*For he knows we are but dust and that our days are few and brief, like grass, like flowers, blown by the wind and gone forever.*"
- Psalm 39:4–5—"*Show me, LORD, my life's end and the number of my days; let me know how fleeting my life is. You have made my days a mere handbreadth; the span of my years is as nothing before you. Everyone is but a breath, even those who seem secure.*"

When we are suffering and feeling the crushing, we often feel the temptation to buck up and seem strong, capable, and fine. But if we are humble and honest, we actually feel tender and fragile. In partnership with our new wineskin of honesty, might we just be frank about our fragility? Our fragility gives room for a fresh filling.

Not only is this beneficial for us, but I believe it is what the next generation and the world are looking for, an honest and relatable follower of Christ that is just as fragile as them but walking confidently in truth and empowered by the Spirit. Is Jesus really gentle and humble at heart for fragile folks like us? If you do not live into this reality, what will be your witness to those who feel this so fully? The reality is . . .

There is humbling freedom in our fragility.

We see the power of human fragility lived beautifully by God incarnate, Jesus. Almost every climatic part of Jesus' ministry has something to do with the confusing fragility of God and man—and Jesus, allowing Himself to feel and experience "weakness." The fragility of the incarnation moves us during Christmas and allows us to delight in Jesus coming in flesh, as a baby, in a humble place to parents who were unprepared and . . . fragile. Jesus weeping over His friend Lazarus is not the picture of an action movie hero with a chiseled chin and paralyzed tear ducts. Jesus' honesty and fragility in the Garden of Gethsemane is a humble and powerful picture of our Savior before the climax of His ministry, the cross. The cross, naked and broken, is permission for us to be fragile. Even in the moments of the cross, people jeered at His fragility and invited Him to use all of His power and strength to call down angels to save Him, but *no, He is fragile on that cross and dies for you and me.* As He rises and meets with His disciples, He takes another step of fragility by entrusting a prized possession and priority, His mission, to ordinary men and women like you and me. Like handing your child your great-grandma's cherished china, the fragility of what Jesus was handing to people like you and me is quite captivating. It is humbling. As you explore and express your fragility, here are some things that help remind me of own my fragility:

- Keep the Sabbath…feel your limits, cease, delight in the Lord, and worship Him regularly.
- Stretch and feel the limits, aches, and pains while taking some deep breaths to feel your capacity.
- Fast from something—I usually bounce between my phone or food—and experience the fragility while focusing on Jesus.
- Nap…acknowledge your need for rest and close your eyes.
- Meet with a counselor and be honest. Admit that you need support.

LAMENT

I have to be honest, when I first read a book on true lament, I cursed out loud. I know we just spoke about honesty, but I don't want to tell you which word I said. I had many reasons to lament but like a muscle you just never use, it was a resource and point of deep intimacy with God I just left in the Bible and put on a shelf. Lament is a pretty spiritual, Christianese word. Mark Vroegop, in his book *Dark Clouds, Deep Mercy*, defines it as, "the honest cry of a hurting heart wrestling with the paradox of pain and the promise of God's goodness."[2]

It's the honest cry of, "God you could have _____!" "Why did you let _____ do that to me!?" and "What were you thinking…"

As Vroegop beautifully explains, "Lament stands in the gap of pain and promise," and "lament is prayer in pain that leads to trust."[3] This is the humbling work of the Christian who bravely says that it does not line up, that you don't get it, maybe even that you do not agree, while making the fragile and honest effort to stay close to Jesus.

Lament is the gift God gives us to steward the crushing. Without it, all the new wine will be tainted or contaminated by things like spiritualization, hiddenness, bitterness, and even toxic religion. It takes a lot of humility and honesty to lament as you are staying at the table for the hard conversations and taking the "second seat," recognizing that He is God and you are not. It's the humbling and honest work to possibly land at disagreement but still choosing to believe He and His promises are true.

In *Suffering*, Paul David Tripp names a sad reality: "Many Christians never just suffer the thing they are suffering but also suffer *the way* they suffer that very thing." I believe a key way that Christians suffer and miss out on new wine and wineskins that come from crushing is pride. We must be honest in our lament and, y'all, we all have plenty of reasons to lament.

Lamentation is not a prescription to humility, nor is it a step-by-step process to suffer well, but it does keep you tethered intimately with the One who does heal and humble us, Jesus. Bring your pain, not your pride, as you engage God in this new wineskin.

VULNERABLE COMMUNITY

It is really easy to be "humble" if you never interact with anyone. If you never have anyone to compare and compete with, humility ain't that bad. If no one pushes your buttons, asks anything of you, or acknowledges an accomplishment of theirs or yours, we can stay pretty low.

The Benedictine monks, a community pursuing and marked by godliness and humility, have twelve steps of humility. I do think humility might be easier in community, but the reality is that most people reading this book are not considering, or living within, monastic community and have certain hurdles to radical humility in different areas of their lives. Vocation, family, hobbies, social media, and more all tempt us away from humility. So what do we do if we don't want to run off to be monks or nuns?

I believe a new wineskin for the new wine created in the crushing is a refreshment of an authentic and vulnerable community. The crushing and isolation is not a good mix, especially in your pursuit of tender humility. John Wesley, the founder of the Methodist movement, borrowed and adopted the practice of "bands" from the Moravians. These bands are small groups of three to five people who are pursuing being fully known by one another through prayer, reading, and confession. The band model has benefitted me, and generations of Christ followers, in our pursuit of being more like Christ.

The band that I am a part of submits to a series of questions on a biweekly basis, which are:

- How is it with your soul?

- What are your struggles and successes?
- How might the Word and Spirit be speaking in your life?
- Do you have any sin to confess?
- Is there anything you desire to keep secret? Or even spicier…did you just lie to us about anything?

As these questions show, a vulnerable community is not rocket science nor a perfect template to follow, but this might be a new wineskin that you need to say yes to. If you read this and say, "Well, I don't have those people in my life! What do I do?" first, I want to acknowledge that loneliness is real and difficult, especially in a season of crushing…almost unbearable. Second, I would love to put my hands on your shoulders, look you in the eyes, and encourage you to maybe check out a church near you. The Church is God's plan A in His mission and, therefore, your formation that happens in partnership with the Spirit.

TRAVAILING PRAYER

There is something unique about the prayers of someone who has been crushed and pressed. The travailing prayer, when your ego and "politeness" have been crushed through circumstances, suffering, and pain, is a powerful new territory to explore. It is new ground that I am still exploring with the help of a guide in my life, Dr. Thomas, who lives in the reality of gritty and fierce prayer, which he calls travail. Travailing prayer is a step away from casual and polite prayer toward laborious and unhindered prayer, like childbirth. This is the powerful prayer that Isaiah speaks of in Isaiah 62:7: "give him no rest…" It feels almost offensive and uncomfortable, at least for me, but since losing my daughter and processing my disappointment, failures, and trauma in deeper ways…I find myself bouncing in between resting in the beauty of liturgy and monastic practices and letting myself fully go into messy, fierce, travailing prayer. I can sit still in my blue chair and engage in prayer, but I can also go to my closet (which my daughter calls my crying and yelling closet) and go to war. This was not the case prior to my real crushing season, but it is a new wineskin for the new wine of intimate trusting prayer.

Luke 9:37–43 shows this way of praying that expresses our heart to Jesus. In this story, a *dad of a demon-possessed son calls out* among a large crowd that came to meet Jesus. When I read this entire passage, I can imagine this brokenhearted and desperate father pushing through a crowd and crying out to "ask" in a way that was different from how he had asked before. The *dad begs for his son*—let me say it again, *begs* for Jesus to help. This father *did not have ego in this interaction, just desperation and total reliance on Jesus to help*. And how did Jesus respond? He healed the boy and gave the healed son back to the father.

This is a new way to pray, a new way for us to pray, as we are crushed and pressed. This sort of travailing prayer would be like a woman travailing in childbirth, depicted in Elijah's prayer posture in 1 Kings 18:42 when he climbed to the top of Mt. Carmel, bowed low, and prayed with his face between his knees. This sort of prayer is like the undignified prayers of Hannah, being mistaken for drunk babbling by the priest Eli, praying for a child in 1 Samuel 1:12–16. Praying louder and more wild, with fits and tears, does not mean you are travailing.

These prayers are humble and hungry prayers, gritty and lowly prayers with full knowledge of their own limits but also confident in the limitless God who is listening. Travailing prayer is the language of a disciple going through crushing.

I am still in process and longing for deeper and more free moments of ruthless and fragile prayers of travail. As I have wrestled and longed for a humble and hungry prayer life, I have had to ask for God to crush my ego and religion, my politeness and concern for reputation and appearance, and He has done that often by breaking my heart for a specific reason. Of course, my heart was broken for my wife and daughter and I prayed differently for them. As I think about the next generation, the church, or even my family that has yet to meet Jesus, I pray differently. But as we long for the new wineskin of travail, might you ask for your heart to break. This requires (oh my... looky here) honesty and fragility leading to a period of deep lament.

Through your humbling, in the crushing, what has the Spirit broken your heart for and how might you adopt a new way to pray?

OBSCURITY & HIDDENNESS

How do you make wine? Crushing grapes and time. How do you make fresh oil? Pressing olives and purifying them. When it comes to making wine, not only is there the painful separation of the wine and the skins, but then that juice is set aside, in obscurity for a time, to ferment. Then there is something sacred about that obscurity and hiddenness that the new wine experiences. In fact, the longer a wine is set aside to age, the greater it becomes to enjoy. After the crushing, the wine is hidden in obscurity while God is creating the new wine. This is important for multiple reasons, but two in particular: (1) Some of it is messy and needs to be stewarded delicately and (2) the hiddenness and intimacy protects and aids in the process. Both of these reasons highlight the potential difficulty we have in understanding the process fully, honoring the process entirely, or even really interacting with it in awareness.

Hiddenness is the secret sauce of formation in humility. If pride enjoys a platform, humility loves hiddenness.

Like making wine, separating the juice from the skins, and setting it aside to ferment, the process of pressing olives is also something that we can learn from. The weight of the press, in biblical times a humongous stone, pulverizes the pulp and pit of the olive while precious oil dribbles out and is collected. The oil, especially if it is being used for honorable purposes like anointing, is not mixed with anything else. It's kept as pure as can be even if diluting it or mixing it with olive oil from another location might make it easier and more productive. Pressing and purity go hand in hand for the new oil… especially the new oil for anointing. How might we carry our pressing in such a way that we are purified, set apart, in the process?

As we are a part of a new wine movement, like I imagine you are longing for, and desperately needing a fresh anointing for what's ahead, whether you realize it or not, might we remember the following…

Humility is formed in the hidden places and expressed in the public places. When it might get celebrated in the public places, you must return to the hidden places to hand it all back to Jesus in gratitude.

How might purposeful obscurity and hiddenness aid in the fermentation and purification of this moment you are in? As you explore new rhythms of obscurity and hiddenness, here are some suggestions for where to start:

- Select times of silence or possibly practicing a silent retreat.
- Make some courageous boundaries with your phone and social media.
- Create a space where you can close a door behind you, to meet with Jesus in prayer.
- Have a regular rhythm of serving with no one needing to know about it.

There might be more or totally different new practices, new wineskins, for you to explore as you steward the new wine being created in the crushing. In our chase of Christ-like humility, it's worth reorienting our lives and befriending these new wineskins. The crushing is not a season to avoid but to lean into and steward sensitively, led by the Spirit that is advocating, helping, and comforting you in your journey toward greater humility.

LAMENT IN THE CRUSHING

Suffering is hard, especially when we don't have language or understanding about how to do it biblically...or even just "well." The Book of Lamentations invites us to examine our unsatisfied and unfinished stories while still clinging to Jesus and trusting in Him. This requires humility. We spoke of lament as one of the new wineskins to steward in the crushing. Mark Vroegop coaches us brilliantly in his important book *Dark Clouds, Deep Mercy* by offering us simple steps to practice.

1. **Turn and talk to God**—In the crushing, pick humility and honor Jesus by not turning away. Look at your compassionate, gentle, and humble Savior and talk to Him honestly. Check this out in Psalm 77:1–3 (ESV):

   I cry aloud to God, aloud to God, and he will hear me. In the day of my trouble I seek the Lord; in the night my hand is stretched out without wearying; my soul refuses to be comforted. When I remember God, I moan; when I meditate, my spirit faints.

   If these verses feel too messy and offensive, remember, this is the Word of God.

2. **Complain**—The honest and humble person knows their place and God's and does not hold back their complaint. God, in all of His compassion, is not squishy and weak but strong and capable to take your complaint. Read Psalm 13:1–2 (ESV).

   How long, O LORD? Will you forget me forever? How long will you hide your face from me?

   How long must I take counsel in my soul and have sorrow in my heart all the day?

   How long shall my enemy be exalted over me?

   Heads-up—as this is written, God does not gasp nor thunder from the throne "How dare you, you little punk!" There is a rooted, consecrated confidence and apparent trust in this complaint. The reality is, in the crushing, humble and messy prayers are always better than silent suffering and despair.

3. **Ask**—I want you to first read Psalm 12:3–4 (ESV):

   Consider and answer me, O LORD my God; light up my eyes, lest I sleep the sleep of death, lest my enemy say, "I have prevailed over him," lest my foes rejoice because I am shaken.

   Why don't we, in the crushing, ask God? I will go first. Why don't I ask every time I feel crushed? I am afraid He will be mad with me, I feel like I am bothering Him, I am concerned I will be seen as weak so won't be entrusted with something, or I just don't deserve the answer. But I believe I can take those very reasons to the Lord and experience greater freedom and boldness to humbly steward the crushing. Remember, He knows how fragile we are and He has not come to make us superheroes, but redeemed jars of clay.

4. **Trust**—Humble lament cannot end in venting. In your humility, you raise the white flag and acknowledge that you are human and He is God, so you will take a step toward trust in His promises and trustworthiness. Psalm 13:5–6 (ESV) is a great example of this.

   But I have trusted in your steadfast love; my heart shall rejoice in your salvation. I will sing to the LORD, because he has dealt bountifully with me.

   Consider the practice of lament by following those steps. Possibly on a napkin in the coffee shop you're sitting in, on a page in your journal, or on the notes app on your phone. Let's learn the humbling and powerful art of lament.

———————————

Lord, in the crushing would we feel Your presence and kindness. In our pressing, would we experience You sitting with us like a friend in a waiting room. Teach us to handle our brokenness, our crushing, like You would. And Jesus, if any of this is just words on pages typed by Zach with no Kingdom purpose, help the reader forget them! BUT if any of these things might encourage and equip my new friend reading and produce fruit in their lives, let it be so. Amen.

section two

Expressing Humility

Chapter 5

Creature

"Humility is the consent of the creature
to let God be all."

ANDREW MURRAY

For he knows how we are formed,
he remembers that we are dust.

PSALM 103:14

On day three of the Outpouring, I jumped onstage (no time to go around to the stairs when the manifest presence of God had arrived) and I hit my shin hard on the side of the stage. I grumbled a not so holy word, then led prayer...but I had an ugly bruise and minor limp for a couple days.

We went through pounds and pounds of wintergreen mints because when you sing, pray, preach, and so on, your breath can stink. On my way to the bathroom, people would stop me and ask me to pray, sometimes even while I was in the bathroom...but I really had to go. We quickly began to feel our limits and would think about our pace and its sustainability. We needed to think about our families and everyday responsibilities: paying our bills, answering emails, getting enough sleep, and drinking enough water. As God was pouring out His Spirit in power and peace and the world began to notice, key leaders realistically had to take nights off to put their kids to bed, throw a makeshift birthday party for a son who had flown in, and for me, take my girls on a date. I learned that even though God was moving supernaturally and we could rest in the Holy Spirit's fresh filling and leadership, we were human. We were so human...but so in awe of what God was doing in our midst. Our feet hurt, we had sore throats, we were tired and sometimes short-tempered...but God was pouring out.

The first night, I remember the piles of cheap pizzas that arrived to feed the students who had stayed or come back to the chapel. We needed food.

A freshman brought a Keurig and boxes and boxes of Keurig cups and created a free coffee station for those coming to worship and those serving. We were sleepy and needed caffeine.

At one point Chick-fil-A came to our rescue to design our lines (make sense, right?) and the Salvation Army provided food and porta-potties. We desperately needed their help.

The reality is that there are many people, dear brothers and sisters of mine, who served and led in impactful ways that you will never know about. It was heroic, beautiful, and overwhelmingly human all at the same time. We had not become superheroes at Asbury; we were and still are fragile vessels...just dust, vapors, or clay. There is something so important in our pursuit of Christ-like humility in that we have such a correct picture of who we are, how we are made, and what we deeply need in comparison to and in deep intimate union with God.

The fact is, when we forget we are creatures, we get cocky.

If we forgot that we are simply creatures, created by God, we begin to strive and try to control. Being a created being, a creature, does not mean that we are a worm or puppet, but it does place us in our correct position and role, especially when we might be tempted to grab the reins. What happened at Asbury was definitely a situation that tempted many to jump in a captain's seat, and if and when that occurred, it was clear we were veering away from the greatest impact in the encounter. We were creatures encountering the Creator and it wasn't humiliating; it was awe-inspiring and humbling.

CREATUREHOOD

Andrew Murray, in his foundational book *Humility: The Journey Toward Holiness*, paints the perfect picture of the reality that we are creatures and until we understand it and rest in it, we will not experience real humility.

The call to humility has been too little regarded in the Church because its true nature and importance have been too little apprehended. It is not something that we bring to God, or that He bestows; it is simply the sense of entire nothingness that comes when we see how truly God is everything. When the creature realizes that this is a place of honor, he consents to be—with his will, his mind, and his affections—the vessel in which the life and glory of God are to work and manifest themselves; he sees that humility is simply acknowledging the truth of his position as creature and yielding to God His place.

We realize, as Genesis 3:19 tells us, from dust we came and to dust we will return. To express humility is to understand the reality of who we are. Creatures. Created by God to glorify Him and enjoy Him.

Adam was created first from dust and the breath of God, and then Eve through the rib of Adam. Created beings to glorify and delight in the Creator. When we step out of that beloved identity and begin to think more of ourselves, we step into areas of pride and entitlement. Pride, the release of humility, is then the root of all sin and brokenness. Satan and the fallen angels picked pride and they fell from heaven. The serpent in the garden convinced Eve that she knew better than God, and via pride, sin entered our lives. When we think we know better, that we have something on or over the Creator, we find ourselves in the toxic seat of pride. The world tells us that to settle into this reality and live within our limits is to subdue ourselves, relinquishing our desire to achieve and make a mark. The reality is that from this place we experience greater intimacy with the Creator who is in charge. A deep understanding of our creaturehood is not one that leads us to live like worms, just pieces of junk that got lucky via Jesus, but actually to an immense chase after restful lowliness. In a world marked by "FOMO," the desire for followers and prestige just confronts us with the reality of our limits, capacities, and boundaries, which actually offers us restful peace. When the world says hustle, our humble Savior invites us to go lower with Him.

Not only is there rest as we settle into our creaturehood, but there's an open door to living under the power of the cross, reliant on Jesus and His power for all things. No résumé, crown, or secret skill sheds the reality that we are human, created by God. Humility and humanity should go hand in hand, but in this cultural moment, it does not always equal up. Culture tells us to live into our humanity and conquer, explore, and write our own story. The Creator invites us to rest, rely, and live out His story. The lack of our understanding of correct position in the story results in brokenness, both in self and in culture, and striving outside of our God-given talents.

RECOVERING "EPIC CHRISTIANS"

With a dear friend, I recently have been discussing the churches and Christian culture we grew up in in the mid-2000s. Nothing less than epic Christianity was permissible in our eyes. We practiced spiritual things that at face value are not bad but, in fact, beautiful and honoring to the heart of God: praying through the night, fasting for weeks, ministering in the least reached and most dangerous places, worshipping, preaching and reaching hundreds, and more. These things were *it* for us. Not only did we live for these things, but we followed leaders who seemingly knew nothing less in the Christian journey as well.

To be Christian was to be epic. It permeated all of our language, all church branding at the time (just think of some of the youth group names you heard from the 1990s and 2000s), and the books we read. Martyrs, megachurch pastors, and superstar worship leaders were what we watched. Monks, lay leaders, generous and godly businessmen, faithful Bible teachers, parents who led their homes well in honoring the Lord, those seemed like JV compared to platforms, sweet haircuts, deep V-neck T-shirts, and more. This was not only how we saw following Jesus exteriorly, but the "epic-ness" of following Jesus flowed inside and was all over our individual practices and prayer lives. This created a euphoric, at times, faith that felt more like high highs and low lows over time.

But we did not learn about our limits. We did not pause to read about practices like Sabbath, celebration, Christian friendship, and more. We had not owned our humble humanity, so we created an unrealistic, and definitely unsustainable, template of what following Jesus looks like, which leads to feeling defeated and disappointed. That has led many to throw up their arms and pull away from their faith altogether. Instead of examining the unrealistic expectations through a biblical lens, and not Christian culture's, we tap out and make an agreement that something must be wrong with us or our faith. This is defeating and running rampant among many.

In my years of ministry, inside and outside of the local church, I have also walked with many young men who struggle with purity and married couples who struggle with intimacy. Almost every time, the destructive and deceptive presence of porn is part of the story. Porn confuses our sexuality and perverts our intimacy. Real-life intimacy, the beautiful and vulnerable aspects of intimacy, are tossed to the side in porn and blown up to be epic and intense. Porn convinces the participant of a lie that not only impacts them in a moment but rewires so much mentally, emotionally, and physiologically. Usually, it whispers "you are in control" and "you are due 100 percent consumer satisfaction," which does not compute with godly, humble, mutually submissive intimacy in marriage. Many couples or individuals I meet with then struggle with the real, normal, honest expressions of intimacy. It's beautiful but different... leaving them sometimes disappointed, confused, or frustrated. It can feel unsatisfactory, so they keep engaging in porn to get that intense hit while trying to be faithful in the ordinary, natural, and sweet real-life relationship they cherish.

I believe many people have walked away from real-life relationships with God and the Church because they were introduced to an unrealistic, epic, unsustainable, intense, and glorified consumeristic Christianity. Spiritual porn instead of deep and meaningful Christian spirituality. They get to be in control, they get 100 percent "satisfaction," and anything less is not up to their standards and does not meet their needs. It's the slow, chilly, quiet mornings with Jesus before our kids wake up and interrupt that don't seem as holy and impactful as stages, prayer nights, and prophetic words. But Christianity is epic because of the Creator, not the creature.

The gritty faith practices of studying the Word, sharing the faith, showing up and being honest in an accountability group, and getting to church on Sunday seem to pale in comparison to what they had imagined. The number of times I have opened up the Word and spent time in prayer and did not receive a download from heaven or weep through a psalm far outnumbers the moments that those things have occurred. Might we reclaim the ordinary and simple intimacy with Jesus that occurs in blue chairs in our living rooms, kitchen tables before the sun rises, prayer closets that no one knows about, and little sweet conversations in coffee shops?

Am I saying that you and I are not invited to exciting encounters with God and impactful adventures in His mission? No. Am I against zeal or even a bit of reckless abandon for His name? No. But when the epic supersedes the eternal, when the shine overshadows the sacrifice, or the outpouring makes the ordinary seem like a waste of time, we can get lost and jaded quickly. The peculiar reality is that when you are submitted to your Savior and He asks you to go to the ends of the earth, lead worship and prayer through the night, *experience a supernatural outpouring*, or stand in front of tens of thousands to share about Jesus, it does not seem so epic in the midst of it but quite ordinary…faithful…intimate…real. A creature, a fragile jar, being led by and utilized by the Creator.

To this day, the reality of being a recovering "epic Christian" is a regular topic of conversation with my friend and my dear counselor. We should go to the least reached and far-off places, we are invited to engage in enduring prayer and worship, the practice of fasting, preaching, leading, and more are all gifts from God that we receive and serve out of but we must not forget that we are creatures, not superheroes. My counselor often has to remind me…

Christ did not come to cancel our creaturehood but to redeem it.

We are creatures and not the Creator. This Truth serves us in our everyday life along with tender times of grief, disappointment, and more. When we get this wrong, usually with religiously acceptable titles or even Christianese sayings that are celebrated, we live outside of our limits and can burn out and live in pride. This does not lead us to flopping and flimsy faith, though. Accuracy in our assessment of self does not have to lead to passivity or lack of confidence. Clarity is kind and when we aren't clear with ourselves, we set ourselves up poorly. In this, don't shrink back and appear weak or wimpy. I have to remind myself often, the opposite of pride is not pushover.

With consecrated confidence and Spirit-fueled humility, we can live into the simple reality that it is not us but the One living and leading through us, the Creator of all things, who is moving and partnering with us.

One of the most "epic Christ followers" in history, the apostle Paul, writes in his first letter to the Corinthians about his limits, simplicity, and creaturehood in chapter 2, verses 1–5:

"And so it was with me, brothers and sisters. When I came to you, I did not come with eloquence or human wisdom as I proclaimed to you the testimony about God. For I resolved to know nothing while I was with you except Jesus Christ and him crucified. I came to you in weakness with great fear and trembling. My message and my preaching were not with wise and persuasive words, but with a demonstration of the Spirit's power, so that your faith might not rest on human wisdom, but on God's power."

In Paul's humility, he rested in the reality of his creaturehood and preached Jesus free of any woo, charisma, and addition. Doesn't that sound nice? There is freedom in remembering that *God is delighted to call you Son and Daughter, not Superman and Wonder Woman.*

From a "recovering epic Christian," here are some concepts that might help you meditate and take inventory of how you are doing in your "recovery":

- **Sobriety**—Sobriety is simply being clear, in our right mind of understanding, and thoughtful.

When we lose sobriety and become drunk on the big, flashy, epic, and sparkly...we lose ourselves and can quickly detach from intimacy with Jesus for things like religion, striving and hustle, and slip into pride and self. When we pursue sobriety, a key topic in wisdom literature, we stay aware of who we are and who He is. Sobriety is not that Debbie Downer friend trying to slow you down but an anchor, offering us full perspective and keeping us low. Humility and sobriety are a match made in heaven, literally.

What resources and practices keep you sober minded?

- **Limits**—Are you aware of your limits? Self-awareness is one of the most undervalued and underutilized concepts in our Christian walk. As we grow in awareness of our own limits, holistically, we can stay in our lanes in following Jesus and making Him known. With that truth, we can celebrate guardrails and thrive within the limits He has created for us. Follow His lead in your limits.

  How are you feeling about your limits, strengths, weaknesses, and your current assignment from the Lord?

- **Faithful**—I grew up playing soccer, and whenever I would play basketball, in real life or on a video game console, I would get anxious and frustrated. My gauge of success, my scorecard, was wrong for the game I was playing. When it comes to "epic Christianity," our scorecards can be skewed and out of place, which then stirs up emotions, causes us to start hustling and striving, and comparison and competition can bubble up. Our scorecard should be centered in faithfulness, which is our ultimate goal and what we hope to hear one day: "Well done, good and faithful servant."

What is your definition of faithfulness in your Christian walk? Is it biblical or cultural?

Have you held an example, a Christian leader or church, as the pinnacle or goal instead of or over a scriptural mandate or teaching of faithfulness and impact? Who? How so? Why? What might you do about that?

- **Pace**—There is something so healthy about pace when it comes to our humanity. I cannot move at the same speed of an Olympic track runner, nor can I keep up with emails, texts, and calls like a top-tier stock exchange guru. I just know myself. How about you? Not only does pace keep us safe and healthy, but it offers us endurance and the possibility of a long, faithful, and fruitful journey. When it comes to Jesus, following Him faithfully, and making an impact for the Kingdom, He'd like to partner with you long-term and not just for a sprint. We see the mystery of pace and the importance of season throughout Christ's teaching, especially in all the agricultural examples that are used. A humble person is comfortable with a Christ-paced life.

What pace of life feels authentic to self and faithful to Jesus' leadership in your life?

What practices, people, and rhythms aid in your pursuit of pace in your life?

- **Friendship**—John 15:15 reminds us that we are no longer slaves or servants but friends. When I am with a friend, I do not need to be impressive, epic, or prove my worth. When I am with a friend, I am at peace and enjoying the companionship. Sometimes, in the midst of friendship, there are adventures that blow you away and you exert all your energy. Sometimes, in friendship, you slow way down, take a seat, wait and listen. *It does not really matter what you do with a friend because real friendship isn't based on activity, it's based on identity.* The more I spend time with a friend, I usually look more, act more, and sound more like him or her. Friendship with Jesus is a fast track to humility. Enjoy it.

    What is your relationship with a local body of believers, the church, as you engage in other expressions of your faith?

    What does God say about you? Not the Enneagram, your employer, your spouse, a BuzzFeed quiz, or your social media followers/likes.

I believe what God did at Asbury offered a new narrative of what is really available for very ordinary and unremarkable places and people. Does what God did at Asbury disqualify or sideline the Christian influencer or "celebrity," shut down beautiful production and laser lights, or exceptional preaching and teaching…absolutely not. Praise God it does not. God is doing a new thing but in that new thing, He is in charge…maybe it's an expansion, not exclusion. Possibly an invitation to be laterally postured and for hope to rise in all expressions instead of hierarchical and "come and see." I don't know…remember, I preached a "stinker" and hoped to get home for a nap.

CELEBRITIES?
THEY ARE JUST CREATURES

At the end of *The Hobbit*, after Bilbo's epic journey that must have produced a little clout in the Shire, like a local celebrity who takes some pride in his escapades, there is a precious and invaluable interaction between Bilbo and his dear friend Gandalf. After his journey with the dwarfs, confronting a dragon, and finding that precious ring, he might feel pretty impressive. Bilbo spoke about the prophecies that their adventure had seemingly proven true and Gandalf wisely humbled the adventuresome hobbit, finishing with this meaningful interaction.

"You are a very fine person, Mr. Baggins, and I am very fond of you, but you are only quite a little fellow in a wide world after all."

"Thank goodness!" said Bilbo, laughing, and handed him a tobacco jar.

Bilbo had done something heroic, but he was still just a "little fellow in a wide world after all." In the conversation of creatures and Creator, and our pursuit of the Christian virtue of humility, we have to explore the topic of Christian celebrities, influencers, and more. There is so much discussion around this topic and in the midst of Asbury's experience in February, many folks noted the complete ordinariness and simplicity of what was going on. Concepts like "anti-celebrity" and "nameless and faceless" were used and have been, I've noticed, used more and more since in narrating what we experienced at Asbury and in other contexts now. How do we engage this while also not poking at our dear brothers and sisters with platforms, titles, and other achievements that place them in categories that culture elevates and separates? *Aren't they just creatures too?*

The reality is that the body of Christ is made up of many parts, as 1 Corinthians 12 tells us, and in Romans 12 we see the different gifts being expressed and complementing one another. In the image of the body, in Corinthians, we are encouraged not to compare and compete nor state that one body part is more valuable than the other. In Romans 12, it is stated simply,

"For just as each of us has one body with many members, and these members do not all have the same function, so in Christ we, though many, form one body, and each member belongs to all the others. We have different gifts, according to the grace given to each of us" (Romans 12:4–6a).

How do these two passages impact the way we see our teammates, other parts of the body, that seem to express themselves on stages and other platforms? How can I judge a toe that happens to be a toe in front of ten thousand people every Sunday? Do I immediately write off an ear that has a hundred thousand followers on TikTok? Or do I give less time to a finger that doesn't have a social media following but is a faithful father and employee? In the context of these passages, we are confronted by our judgment of others. Praise God for stadiums that are filled with fog, laser lights, speakers, and zeal, and praise God for neighborhood churches, living rooms, and great small groups. They are not competing; they are expressing themselves. Are there unique expectations and unique challenges because of different contexts and expressions? One hundred percent.

Are there real distractions? *Yes.*

Are there greater temptations? *Definitely.*

Can it automatically be written off as sin and broken? *I don't think so.*

But instead of judging, ranking, and more…let us be driven to humble prayer and intercession for one another. I wonder, as co-creatures doing our best to follow and submit to the Creator, how might God bless and move in our midst if we cheered on and prayed for each other in our journeys toward greater Christ-likeness, like Romans 12 and 1 Corinthians 12 encourage us? The sad reality is that in the Western Church, we have stories upon stories of platformed Christian brothers and sisters "failing" in their public ministry. *The Church is sick of highlight reels that compensate for dark behind-the-scenes footage.* So, what is the solution? I can't imagine it is to subdue people in their vibrancy and giftedness. I don't think we default to a spiritual "tall poppy syndrome." How might our platforms not be our highlights but our honest lives and authentic stories? This is not a gimmick. *This is humble Christianity.*

An old friend would teach regularly that at the foot of the cross, there is level ground. So, if it is a megachurch pastor, single mom, Grammy Award–winning music artist, retired couple, *New York Times* bestselling author, seasoned youth volunteer, or anyone else…at the foot of the cross our eyes are on Jesus and not sizing each other up on our right and left.

Every person is beautifully, and simply, a creature in the shadow of the cross.

How might we cheer on these fellow brothers and sisters who have different roles in the Church than us? Each of our pursuits toward Christ-like humility look different. The hurdles and temptations, the wins and expressions, all will look different in our very personal journeys with Jesus toward lowliness. Bernard of Clairvaux paints a picture of the unique challenge for the "celebrity" that could make us scoff, like saying "good luck" or soberly pray for our brothers and sisters in Christ. He says, "It is no great thing to be humble when you are brought low; but being humble when you are praised is a great and rare achievement." As we, as one body with many parts and purposes, pursue greater humility together, I wonder if we could pray and examine our hearts pertaining to each of our platforms and purposes. It does not mean an individual is prideful if their platform is an arena or has tons of followers on social media, nor does it mean someone is humble if their platform seems "less significant" and less far reaching. I imagine you have met multiple examples for both of those scenarios. So, as we all get humble at the foot of the cross, might we examine ourselves and honestly intercede for others in these three possible areas...

- **Posture of the Heart**—What is the posture of your heart pertaining to the platform you have? Is it your family dinner table? Is it your team at work? Is it a class or church body you shepherd? Whether it's wrangling toddlers or posting content to hundreds of thousands, what do you posture with your platform, profile, privileges, and more?
  - *How do you consider the platform and privileges you have? How do you utilize them for your purposes and/versus Kingdom purposes?*

- **Purpose of the Platform**—Without overspiritualizing your platform, whether it's mom, pastor, performer, etc., what do you honestly see as its purpose? How is it purposed in your life? Your vocation? For your affirmation and identity?

  o *Do you purpose your platform for your own gain or for the sake of others?*

- **Practices of the Person**—What are the practices present in your life that help you steward the platform you have with humility? What practices do you have in your life that subdue the victories and failures to not impact your view of self and others?

  o *How do you steward the opportunities you have with practices that resemble Jesus' life on earth like prayer, silence and solitude, team, fasting, etc.?*

Jesus' temptations in the desert[1] now might sound more like "I will make you the greatest influencer of all time!" or "I will put you on the front page of *Christianity Today* or *Outreach* magazine" or "You will have the hottest podcast and your pick to any conference stage." Maybe it's not those things but more close to home: "You'll have the picture-perfect family," "I will give you that promotion," or "Your kid will always make the team and get straight A's." Whatever temptation that catches your eye, Jesus is your friend and is willing to walk you through whatever you face, or you observe others facing. Instead of judging and assuming, let's turn our prayers for the Church, influencers and celebrities and everyone else, to be marked by Christ-like humility for the sake of showing the world Jesus and His Gospel! Maybe you pause now and pray now...

WHO AM I?

Something special about allowing ourselves to be sons and daughters and not superheroes is that we can honestly, without faking it or hiding it, engage with God with our doubts, fears, and questions. When we don't do this, we might in fact be picking pride. We see this authentic faith in many men and women in the Bible, not holding back or putting on a show for God, along with many people faking it, living in bondage, and missing out on real relationships with God. One man asked four questions at a climatic point of his very human story that I think many creatures ask the Creator. Moses, at the burning bush, shows us a template of pursuing humility while being honest and known in all of our humanity.

Moses had a difficult story of being a Hebrew saved from the river, found by the pharaoh's daughter, and raised in an Egyptian court. He also had, in a fit of rage, killed an Egyptian taskmaster and ran away. Moses had gone from the pharaoh's court to the desert... the crushing of riches and ease to sand, dust, walking, sheep was real and at work. Moses was a prepared but very human vessel for this moment. Moses' questions are very human and they are responded to by a very Holy God. Not only at the burning bush but for Moses' entire story, this man of God is so human, such a creature, and experiences the supernatural and the very human aspects of following God. Let's explore and engage the Spirit in how we might be freed up and formed as we engage Exodus 3 and 4 ...

- **"Take off your sandals ... this is holy ground,"** **Exodus 3:5**—Our posture and way we approach

God can strengthen our understanding of who He is and who we are. God's holiness contrasts with our humanity and leads us deeper into humility. As humans, it's good to take off our shoes sometimes and just understand who we are meeting with.

- **"Who am I?" Exodus 3:11–12**—This question, when really open-handed and submitted to God and His answer, is a very honest and human one to ask. God, will you help me understand who I am to be doing such a thing I am doing? There is sobriety in this question. Self-doubt can be paralyzing, while honest sobriety can actually offer very sure footing. The beauty of God's answer to this question can also tell us much about our won journey. God does not answer Moses' question exactly how you'd expect, but in a way that is much more compelling and helpful…God reminds Moses of who God is, the one who was sending him, leading with him, and going before him.

- **"What shall I say?" Exodus 3:13–22**—A question for instruction, "how," is very human when we are facing something that seems bigger than we can handle. The humanity of Moses' question can lead us to asking humble "how" questions. Instead of these questions being rooted in fear and insecurity, might they be rooted in honest and humble curiosity on how to partner with God.

- **"What if…?" Exodus 4:1–9**—This vulnerable question of "what if" is a pure one that I believe the Father in heaven delights in His children asking. God is not wringing His hands and pacing back and forth in His Throne Room. He wasn't during the time of the Egyptians nor is He now. If we approach God in humility and vulnerability, He might respond in a way that gives us confidence in His supernatural power and provision. Moses would see God go above and beyond in his "what if" question. Might we see the same, or at least be settled by the same power, in our very human "what if" questions.

- **"Are you sure?" Exodus 4:10–17**—This is a creature and Creator moment, clear as day. Moses, after asking vulnerable and honest questions, just really was not up for it. "Can you just send someone else, Lord?" is such an honest and raw request, isn't it? How might you be at a similar place? God might send relief in lots of different ways, and in this scenario, Moses was sent a teammate. I think this is a beautiful act that we can rest in on our journeys. Our humanity and honest questions drive us to a need for community and help. Moses would not be able to do this alone…he was too human… but God would send a teammate. Be honest with God in your humanity but be humble in how He responds and provides for you.

Moses is one of many biblical examples of a very ordinary and vulnerable human being used by a very extraordinary and powerful God. As we read these stories, might we rest in the freedom to be human and honest. Humble but hungry to be used by God.

SWEAT AND BLOOD

The important and mysterious theological understanding of Christ being both God and man is one to wrestle with and delight in simultaneously. The reality that Christ was in total control and chose the cross is that much more compelling when we understand that He wasn't some wishy-washy, squishy, unboundaried pacifist. He was not careening toward death on the cross like a car sliding on ice toward a light post. John 10:18 speaks to this when Jesus states, *"No one takes it from me, but I lay it down of my own accord. I have authority to lay it down and authority to take it up again. This command I received from my Father."* In His humanity and deity, held together in His incarnate body, He picked death for us. He also picked service, stickiness, scraped-up knees, and so-so food. Max Lucado wrote a piece on this that I cannot read without tearing up.

"Completely human, completely divine. Angels watched as Mary changed God's diaper. The universe watched with wonder as the Almighty learned to walk. Children played in the street with Him and had the synagogue leader in Nazareth known who was listening to His sermons...

"Jesus may have had pimples. He may have been tone-deaf. Perhaps a girl down the street had a crush on Him or vice versa. It could be that His knees were bony. One thing's for sure: He was, while completely divine, completely human. For thirty-three years He would feel everything you and I have ever felt. He felt weak.

He grew weary. He was afraid of failure. He was susceptible to wooing women. He got colds, burped, and had body odor. His feelings got hurt. His feet got tired and His head ached. To think of Jesus in such a light is—well, it seems almost irreverent, doesn't it? It's not something we like to do; it's uncomfortable. It is much easier to keep the humanity out of the incarnation. Clean the manure from around the manger. Wipe the sweat out of His eyes. Pretend He never snored or blew His nose or hit His thumb with a hammer... But don't do it. For heaven's sake, don't. Let Him be as human as He intended to be. Let Him into the mire and muck of our world for only if we let Him in can He pull us out."[2]

How might Christ's humanity offer you freedom to feel a bit human? We see the beauty of His humanity when He weeps (John 11:35) over His friend who died, we appreciate His humanity as He napped on a boat (Matthew 8:23–27) and feel His humanity as He sweats and cries in Gethsemane, guarded by His sleeping best friends.

The Garden of Gethsemane is a compelling look into Christ's humanity and prayers. This story is found in Matthew 26:36–46, Mark 14:32–42, and Luke 22:39–46 and it includes some of the most precious moments of Jesus' ministry here on earth. The potential rising in these moments is monumental as it leads to the cross, but the private vulnerability in these moments is just as impactful for you and me. Jesus, in His honesty and rawness, invites His closest three to follow Him deeper into the garden and shares that He is grieved and distressed (Matthew 26:37) to the point of death and asks if they would keep watch. Jesus, in His deity and humanity, gets vulnerable and cries out "Abba," which is an intimate word for "father" like "daddy" or "papa." In His humanity, He needs the closeness of His dad. Jumping to Luke's account of this holy moment, Jesus has a very sober and honest conversation via a question: "If you are willing, remove this cup from Me; yet not My will, but Yours be done." We see Christ's honesty in prayer, His vulnerability and sobriety in His request, and submission to His Father. Christ's creaturehood colliding with His godliness in the Garden of Gethsemane.

Christ as a creature chose to humble Himself so that His Father could use Him to fulfill the salvation of God's children. In His humanity, we see the intertwined God and man authentically conversing with His Abba.

Raw confession and request to His dear friends.

Honest and vulnerable prayer to the Father.

Christ needing to be ministered to by angels as He prayed.

Agonizing in prayer with sweat and blood.

Christ's holiness, Christ's preparation and commission, Christ's creaturehood...all in the garden with Peter snoring in the background. So human and so holy. Christ's humility on display.

A PRACTICE IN ACCELERATING SELF-AWARENESS OF BEING HUMAN

The reason I first got to call Asbury home was that I volunteered as a goalie coach for the men's soccer team. Though I once played and could run, dive, kick, and more...that is not as much the case today. I am quickly humbled and self-aware of my limits when I get to train with the team and take shots on our wonderful goalkeepers. If I need to be reminded to be humble, I just have to start playing with the team.

It is good, in our pursuit of greater humility, to continue to pursue self-awareness in our journeys with Jesus. Our self-awareness might reveal strengths and graces on our lives while also help us grow in understanding of some of our shadows, weaknesses, and struggles. Our humanity becomes much more real as we explore it and pursue self-awareness. As I engage in practices to grow in self-awareness, I have tried to memorize, meditate, and be prompted by Proverbs 20:5. A great passage to explore motives and insight on self and my comfortability to align myself with Christ's description of life in the Kingdom is the Beatitudes in Matthew 5. For the ease of the practice and not being distracted by study and so on, I usually utilize the Message translation of Matthew 5. Here are those two passages...

Proverbs 20:5 reads, *"The purposes of a person's heart are deep waters, but one who has insight draws them out."*

The Beatitudes, found in Matthew 5, from Peterson's *The Message*...

- *"You're blessed when you're at the end of your rope. With less of you there is more of God and his rule."*
- *"You're blessed when you feel you've lost what is most dear to you. Only then can you be embraced by the One most dear to you."*
- *"You're blessed when you're content with just who you are—no more, no less. That's the moment you find yourselves proud owners of everything that can't be bought."*

- *"You're blessed when you've worked up a good appetite for God. He's food and drink in the best meal you'll ever eat."*
- *"You're blessed when you care. At the moment of being 'care-full,' you find yourselves cared for."*
- *"You're blessed when you get your inside world—your mind and heart—put right. Then you can see God in the outside world."*
- *"You're blessed when you can show people how to cooperate instead of compete or fight. That's when you discover who you really are, and your place in God's family."*
- *"You're blessed when your commitment to God provokes persecution. The persecution drives you even deeper into God's kingdom."*
- *"Not only that—count yourselves blessed every time people put you down or throw you out or speak lies about you to discredit me. What it means is that the truth is too close for comfort and they are uncomfortable. You can be glad when that happens—give a cheer, even!—for though they don't like it, I do! And all heaven applauds. And know that you are in good company. My prophets and witnesses have always gotten into this kind of trouble."*

Jesus, help us own our own humanity while also pursuing and submitting to Your restoration and redemption.

Chapter 6

Confidence

The fruit of that righteousness will be peace;
its effect will be quietness and confidence forever.
My people will live in peaceful dwelling places,
in secure homes,
in undisturbed places of rest.

ISAIAH 32:17–18

"There is nothing holy about disagreeing
with what God says about you."

CURT VERNON, MY FRIEND &
ACCOUNTABILITY PARTNER

For sixteen days at Asbury, I sort of felt like a little kid who didn't know any better. You know what I am talking about? When a kid is around their dad, they will do wild things and just assume that their dad will catch them, cover their back, or whatever else. The kid will jump into the pool without warning anyone, jump off the counter with boldness, and flop backward (like one of those summer camp trust-falls) assuming the parent will catch them. There is a radical confidence in the kid because, well, Dad is there.

My youngest, Mercy, is in this season. I have been laughing as I sometimes put her on our kitchen counter when I'm making her bottle or something, and she will just walk right off the counter like Indiana Jones steps onto that invisible bridge in the *Last Crusade*. Bold, risky, and full of confidence. You can judge my parenting, but I think this is really beautiful and she has not fallen to her peril…yet…and I don't think she will. Why? Because her dad is there.

At Asbury, it sort of felt similarly. Because of His apparent presence in our midst, there was a supernatural confidence that came with leading. As I shared in prior chapters, this confidence was not void of difficulty and sanctification, but there was a sort of spiritual swagger to those days. There were moments when I was asked to lead, times that I needed to exercise spiritual authority, moments of pastoring and prayer when I was totally over my head, but I felt the Lord in each one of those moments. I still remember times when I stepped up to the pulpit, not knowing exactly how this would go, and through the Spirit's power and leading, it went all right.

The first time we had a spontaneous reading of Scripture, I joined in. I stepped up and read Isaiah 55, inviting the room to say, "This is the word of God, and we believe it" afterward, and you know what? They followed, someone would spontaneously read out a passage and the room would respond each time, declaring their belief in God's Word. It went on for almost for three hours.

One of the most profound times that I felt God's strength and consecrated confidence was when someone was struggling in the audience. I was not sure exactly what was going on—it was a bowl of spaghetti, spiritual and physical all mixed together—but the surrounding guests didn't seem to be helping. In that moment, I felt the Lord invite me to call them into focus, focus on Jesus, so I asked the room to trust us and to enter back into worship and fix ourselves on why we had all come—encountering and worshipping Jesus. I felt this "whoosh" from my back, like the wind of the Spirit hushing the room and gently grasping their chins to direct their gazes back to Him, away from self or those in the seats. Like a child, I did not know much better... there just was a confidence because the Father was in the room.

One message I shared during those sixteen days came out of Luke 18, verses 15 through 17. In this passage, Jesus invites us into a new way to think about children.

People were also bringing babies to Jesus for him to place his hands on them. When the disciples saw this, they rebuked them. But Jesus called the children to him and said, "Let the little children come to me, and do not hinder them, for the kingdom of God belongs to such as these. Truly I tell you, anyone who will not receive the kingdom of God like a little child will never enter it."

"Anyone who will not receive the Kingdom of God like a little child will never enter it" is a bold and convicting statement. Like many of Jesus' words that cut to the heart, this one seemingly confronts something at our core. Think about how a little child receives things. Pretty straight up, right? When a father shares something with his little child (I'm not talking preteen or young adult), the child believes him. Children don't have cynicism, insecurity, or past disappointments that make them question their father. Kids don't usually "know better" and can be quite naive. They believe most people at their word and it's beautiful. The problem is *sometimes we've grown to "know better."*

God invites us to have childlike confidence, offering to restore it, and to "not know any better."

A lot of times, our childlike confidence is chipped away by pain or pride. Not necessarily big hairy pain or big and hairy pride. It might be "death to childlikeness by 1,000 paper cuts" that makes us "grow up and know better." Pain over time often leads to self-protection. We cast aside our childlike faith because we want to protect the child within us. Our pride tells us that we know better or don't need that childlike faith because we have _____. Fill in the blank with what you place your confidence in: smarts, money, strength, family, health, or whatever you cling to during stress or struggle.

Like Robin Williams in *Hook* when going back to Neverland isn't celebrated and instead of flying, you decide you'll just write a check. You've grown…you're not Peter Pan anymore. In some ways, that is good and right, but Jesus' words in Luke 18:17 still say, *"Truly I tell you, anyone who will not receive the kingdom of God like a little child will never enter it."*

If I could sit across the table from those who have grown

to "know better" because of their pain, I would invite the Spirit to compassionately soften their hearts and peel their fingers away from what they are clinging to so that they welcome openhandedness. I would look at those whose pride has taught them to "know better" and, with an arm around their shoulder, invite them into freedom, possibly sharing Psalm 44:6, "*I put no trust in my bow, my sword does not bring me victory*" or Proverbs 3:26 (ESV), "*for the LORD will be your confidence and will keep your foot from being caught.*" Christ is both compassionate and confrontational, not to humiliate us but to renew our confidence and place it fully and only in Him.

Now please hear me out. I am not asking for unintelligent and blind faith. I am not suggesting that we stuff it down or set things on a shelf and fake it till we make it. I don't think that is biblical confidence, and it doesn't sound like how Jesus would steward our pain or our pride. But I would ask you a question, like I asked students in Hughes Auditorium: "Have you grown to know better?" What would keep you from jumping off the side of the pool, leaping off the counter, or from doing whatever you want to imagine is between you, as His child, and God, your Father?

Since Asbury's sixteen days, I would say I have regained my "don't know better" childlikeness in many ways. I laugh and shrug my shoulders an awful lot more, like a kid saying, "Man, look at my father doing his thing again…and again…and again." There are also times I have been crippled by "knowing better" and chose pain and pride and self-protection, or I fought for "what's mine" or wanted to hide. The pursuit of humility has looked more like me considering two extremes and falling into the ditch of self-deprecation and fear between them.

Consecrated and humble confidence is the freedom and sober moderate middle... It is down the center, though probably with some wobble. I have a doodle like this on a sticky note to remind me of that consecrated humble confidence in the middle...

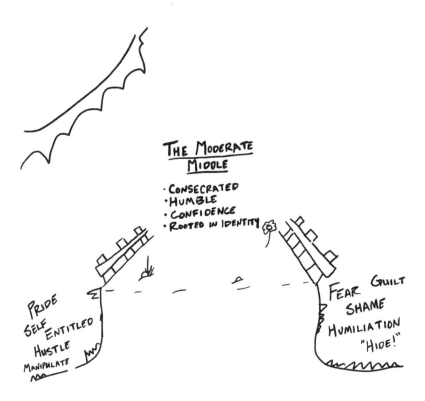

Instead of ending up in one ditch because of the fear of the opposite one, we can walk down the middle with consecrated, humble confidence that is rooted in our identity. We can even, through practices, wisdom, and community, create guardrails that bump us back into the middle and keep us from falling into the ditch. This might all seem too simplified, but I think there is beauty in that Christ-like confidence that comes from identifying humbly with a child. As we pursue greater humility, would we allow Christ to confront our definition of confidence? Would we, in going lower, find ourselves with a renewed sense of consecrated confidence? Would we be found in Christ, crucified and dead to self, and confident in Him?

Going lower in humility will not cancel your confidence. It will consecrate it and set it apart for a greater purpose.

This sort of humble confidence is what we are after. The possibility and expression of humility is a confidence rooted and established by and in Christ, expressed through your consecrated uniqueness, for the sake of His mission and others. It is enjoyed and expressed by a child of God settled in their identity as beloved. Like a child, not knowing better nor building on any pain or pride, their confidence is from the Father and expressed humbly because it is deeply understood that He is the source.

THE PRAYER CLOSET, THE THRONE ROOM, AND THE MORGUE

Some people gain confidence in the gym and others in a classroom or library. A few folks will experience confidence in a boardroom or stadium while others will feel it as they parent, create, move, or chat. Lots of different places can offer us confidence for lots of different reasons. I would like to explore three places that I believe can teach us a lot about a confidence that is unlike any other. Not even a good workout at the gym, a huge sale at your job, or a report card or trophy your kid brings home could compare.

Remember, this is not a self-help book that is designed to help you run up a mountain or through a brick wall by the end of this chapter. I don't have special tricks that will give you swag for your next date nor do I have a formula for you to walk, speak, and think differently. But I do believe that in these places, you will meet with the One who empowers, transforms, and encourages. Without Jesus, these places are just places and these thoughts are just Zach's, mixed up with mentors, author, preachers, and more. I want godly confidence and nothing else. I want a humble confidence rooted in Jesus and empowered by the Spirit, what about you?

Your Prayer Closet

Your prayer closet may not look like a closet, but it is wherever you meet the Lord in private. Before the Lord in intimacy and privacy, honesty and vulnerability, we can be fully seen and hear His voice rooting us in identity. Humble confidence is rooted in Christian identity. One cannot go without the other. This could come from, and be rooted down deep through, preaching, reading, or Christian community, but I believe it is watered and fertilized in our private times with the Lord.

Many of us seem to think of a prayer closet or prayer room as uber spiritual or as a space for introverted Christians. Others might be intimidated, wondering what you do in the prayer closet (like Ricky Bobby not knowing what to do with his hands in front of the camera), and overthink this. My deepest desire is for each one of us to find a space that we can have private and strengthening time with our Friend Jesus, and be comforted and helped by the Spirit. The Father desires to offer you this sort of confidence, but just like I cannot connect with my bride if I run from thing to thing, staring at my phone in between, we must have intentional time with God. I truly believe that renewed, or possibly entirely fresh, confidence is waiting for you.

True humility is real biblical confidence. A real confidence we read about in God's Word and see in the men and women that fill God's Story. As we engage Scripture, we reorient ourselves to the source of our confidence, not just in words or a "holy book," but in God.

How might you lead and live from the prayer closet with humble confidence?

The Throne Room

Possibly the most important context for consecrated and Christ-centered confidence is the Throne Room of God. Because of Christ, we can boldly approach the throne as Ephesians 3:12 tells us: *"In him and through faith in him we may approach God with freedom and confidence."* Hebrews 4:16 invites us to do this as well, *"Let us then approach God's throne of grace with confidence, so that we may receive mercy and find grace to help us in our time of need."* We can confidently enter into the Throne Room and allow God to meet with and consecrate us, setting us and our confidence apart for His purposes.

In biblical times, consecration meant setting something aside with purification for special purposes, sometimes the priests themselves or the tools they would use in the holy places. How might we enter into the Throne Room with confidence, with our whole selves, to be consecrated by the one who sits on the throne, Christ? We can bring along what we glean confidence from—our gifts, dreams, possessions, loved ones, and anyone and anything else—and it will be consecrated in the Throne Room. Submitted to Jesus and in light of His glory and purposes, they will be realigned and reordered in our lives and bring consecrated confidence.

Without the Throne Room, though, we can become too reliant on ourselves, which leads to pride or insecurity. Without consecrated confidence in the Throne Room, we go into the world with what we can bring, believing in our strength. We can go with confidence into the Throne Room. Why? Jesus! We can go out of the Throne Room with confidence. Why? Jesus! When we make an impact and are handed things to grow in confidence *or* when we slip up and lose confidence, where do we go and with whom do we engage? Jesus in the Throne Room.

This might all sound super spiritual and ethereal. Do I have the address for the Throne Room? No, I do not. I realize that it seems a bit full of Christianese, but I do believe this is important.

We have humble confidence in the Throne Room because of the cross of Christ. Without Christ, we cannot go boldly and confidently into the presence of God for conversation, questions, and rest. We would need to rely on our own efforts and righteousness. It would never be enough and it still is not. That is why we need the cross. But because of the cross and our relationship with Jesus, we can go into that glorious place for worship and wonder while also unloading our concerns and crowns. From that place, with rooted identity and consecrated confidence we go into the world, and the door is always open for us to come back with our pride or brokenness to set our eyes on Jesus and cast down our crowns.

During our time at Asbury, my friend David said, "If you could see the altar with spiritual eyes, it would be covered with broken chains." I believe if I could have spiritual eyes to look at the foot of the cross, there would be piles and piles of crowns and résumés. That might need to happen with a nice rhythm for us to continue with humble confidence.

The Morgue

Galatians 2:20 reads, "*I have been **crucified** with Christ and I no longer live, but Christ lives in me. The life I now live in the body, I live by faith in the Son of God, who loved me and gave himself for me.*"

Humble confidence is a crucified confidence. Christ is inviting us to pass through the cross-shaped door into real life with Him, which includes a confident life living under the shadow of the cross and all that entails. This verse has become one of my favorite verses in all of the Bible because of a season in my life where I was absolutely broken, lacking any confidence in myself, and a really skewed understanding of the cross. Earlier on in this book (the doughnut shop), I shared quickly about a season of my life where I lacked confidence and was so troubled with intimidation that I picked old and ugly friends— exaggeration and lying. I had known Christ for multiple years before then, and even though I was on staff at a church, I had flirted with those old friendships that "got me by" when I was afraid and insecure. Because of this, I resigned from the church and found myself in a formal restoration program to process my brokenness and sin patterns. It was beautifully curated with compassion and hope, but I was really broken, embarrassed, and feeling hopeless.

At the church I'd resigned from, there was an elder named Randy who really cared for me well and protected me with Gospel lenses and fierceness for my calling. He did that in lots of ways I will never know but one way was very private and personal. For ninety days straight, like an assignment from the Lord, my friend Randy called me and asked me what Galatians 2:20 said. At first, I would answer with hope for good news and would become grumpy and frustrated when all he had for me was to ask me to recite a verse about being crucified. After the first couple days I had memorized the verse so I could recite it back to him. Once I could do that, he began to ask questions about my weaknesses that had led me to the restoration I was now going through.

After I recited the verse, Randy would ask, "What does that mean? Does that make you a liar?"

Sheesh. That is brutal. In my shame and guilt, I answered this elder of the church, "Well ya Randy, I am a liar... I'm really sorry."

Randy would reply, "You're no liar, Zach. You are a dead man. You've been crucified with Christ."

At first, I was frustrated. But after a bit I understood and began to rest in these phone calls with Randy. His bold proclamation about the crucified life was healing my wounds and giving me consecrated confidence, for the hard work I was doing in my restoration program and for life and ministry. He would ask how I was doing and I'd share about being embarrassed, discouraged, anxious about what would happen next, or afraid of what might happen if I saw someone from that church.

He'd respond, "Well Zach, does a dead man get his feelings hurt?"

Or "Zach, does a dead man get embarrassed?" Or "Zach, are dead men afraid? Sounds like you forgot you were crucified..."

Randy is not a theologian, pastor, conference speaker, or author. He is a roofer, a builder, a husband, father, and prayer warrior. He is heroic (even though he started to "know better") and taught me about how death of self brings confidence in Christ. *When self is crucified, you can have confidence in Christ.* That is why we must understand our place at the morgue. Dead men and women, in Christ, walking in humble confidence.

My friend Christian, a student at Asbury, called Hughes Auditorium "a beautiful graveyard" as he courageously and boldly preached on Galatians 2:20 during the Outpouring. Each seat represented where a person had died, crucified with Christ, and would move forward confidently in Him. Maybe you are reading this at a coffee shop, on an airplane, in your office, or a comfy chair in your home. Look at where you are seated.

It's your gravestone.

You have been crucified with Christ and you no longer live but live this life reliant on the Son of God who died and gave His life for you.

CONVERSATIONS MARKED
BY HUMBLE CONFIDENCE

Have you ever observed a conversation, whether in person or possibly via an interaction online, that is so clearly not marked by humility? What does it sound like? What do you hear between the lines and words? What is the posture of those who are a part of the conversation? How does it leave you or the people feeling? It is really quite moving when you take notice and ask the question of how humility marks interactions. Maybe you sit in a coffee shop and just take note of how folks interact with the baristas while business meetings occur, maybe a first date, or just quick introductions. Often you can notice body language, overhear aspects of the conversations, and even pick up on emotions. Is it not so winsome and encouraging when someone is kind? How great is it when you interact with someone who is just marked by joy and carries themselves with humility? Our humility will of course play out most in our interactions with others. These are opportunities not only to exercise what is in our own hearts, but to witness to Christ's work in our lives and bless others. Our conversations with others—whether those we are close with, those we worship with, or those who disagree with us—all are opportunities from us to represent Christ and His humility in a unique way.

What might be more prominent in public than the antagonists of humility, pride, and selfishness? Christ's humility confronts careerism and status, and His lowliness and gentleness cause friction with "cancel culture" and the harshness we experience in real life and all over social media platforms. What if, instead of flexing our moral uprightness, we chose the lower route, the humbler route, and we confronted pride and sin with humility and gentleness? This sort of humility would tell our story in such a beautiful way. Think about how confrontational and humble Christ was in John 8:1–11. Christ remains calm, gentle in some ways, while being very clear and convicting, He talks to both the Pharisees and woman with humility.

"All right, but let the one who has never sinned throw the first stone!"

And then....

"Where are your accusers? Didn't even one of them condemn you?"

"No, Lord," she said.

And Jesus said, *"Neither do I. Go and sin no more"* (NLT).

The beauty and humility of Christ oozes out of so many interactions and conversations; it's quite moving. In Luke 18, there is a blind beggar who cries out to Jesus on His way, on Mission. The crowd hushes the beggar, but Jesus hushes the crowd. He asks that the blind man be brought to Him and asks kindly, "What can I do for you?"

In Luke 8, a woman who had been declaring herself unclean publicly anytime she went out was determined to get to Jesus. She pushed through the crowd and touched the hem of Christ's robe and was healed from a twelve-year sickness. Jesus was compassionate: "Daughter, your faith has healed you. Go in peace."

Christ's kindness and humility are so compelling to me, especially in John 13 when He interacts with his accuser but does not out him. Judas dips the bread, Satan enters, and Jesus responds by suggesting Judas go and run his errand quickly. Jesus allowed the disciples to come up with their own reasons for their exchange: *"Since Judas had charge of the money, some thought Jesus was telling him to buy what was needed for the festival, or to give something to the poor"* (John 13:29). Talk about humility in conversation...He allows His peers to think He is preparing for a festival (worship) or giving to the poor (charity). Christ's humility is not just ethereal, fluffy, and something to aspire to. It infiltrates and impacts interactions and responses.

Conversations are not off-limits for Christ to invade. In fact, there are many conversations that we could do a better job of inviting Him into. Have you actively asked Jesus to saturate your conversations, whether it's for work or with your family, with His Spirit and character? Could you imagine if you invited Christ's humility and pursued it as you posted, pressed send on emails, or paused and addressed your child when they were misbehaving? I wonder how many times people think about how they are portraying themselves in a meeting or on a date. They want to sound smart, impressive, mysterious, and cool. Could you imagine if we longed for our conversations to be saturated by Christ's lowliness? Not only with fellow believers but waiters or coworkers? Maybe even someone attacking your beliefs or asking a provocative question? Humility never goes out of style, and it paints a uniquely Christ-like portrait to those listening or reading.

A dear friend talks about a specific way he interacts with others that I believe is saturated with Christ-like humility. It is uniquely impactful that this man speaks about this and practices it because he, in many rooms, has the most reasons to make a point in an impressive way. His PhD, lots of experience, a substantial platform, and more would give him plenty of clout to be a somewhat intimidating sage in most rooms. But he challenges many to lean into holy empathetic curiosity.

In the last year or so, after many questions and concerns of how this could be perceived, I have added "empathetic curiosity" to consecration. This is a better descriptor of Christ's curiosity when he speaks with the woman caught in adultery... "Are they still here? Condemning you? No...well me either. Go and sin no more." Consecrated and empathetic.

Many believe that without "consecration," empathy and curiosity could be understood as affirming and encouraging. The reality is, though, that consecrated curiosity on its own can seem judgmental, nosy, or harsh. So combining both, and adding some curiosity, is a powerful tool in humble conversation. In these sorts of humble conversations, you might hear things like...

- That must be really hard.
- Can you help me understand that?
- Would you be okay if I asked another question about that?
- How can I be a good friend to you in this?
- I am sorry.
- I'm honored you'd share that with me.
- Of course, thank you for letting me know how I can honor your boundaries.
- I don't agree, but I want to know more.

We believe that clarity and convictions are kind or humble. So much of culture tells us differently and it keeps us from being clear and differentiated in our beliefs. In humility, we can stand up strongly for our convictions while offering respect and kindness. With humility, there is space for two or more in a conversation to disagree, connect, and be kind. When pride and fear enter in, it is much harder. Humility does not require you to be friends, but it does hold you to a standard of character though. This is important in times of great tension (elections, war, cultural moments, etc.) and among more turbulent and volatile contexts like social media or others. In all of this we must ask, *What if Christians were known by our humility?*

REDEFINING CONFIDENCE

Have you ever seen someone or met someone who totally redefines confidence? They certainly have it and it's captivating, but it's just not what you thought it would be. It's not high-school QB and prom-king energy nor is it nice-suit, nice-car, nice-hair swagger. I have a dear friend who exudes godly confidence and when you see her, you know it. It's otherworldly. But it's so real and it has been cultivated with Christ in beautiful ways. She is a mother to approximately fifty children, all from India. She has seen God move miraculously and she has been deeply disappointed. She has handled both with beautiful confidence rooted in Christ-like humility. I so appreciate her because she redefines confidence in light of humility... in light of Jesus.

Paul gives a great redefinition for expressing confidence in his letter to the Philippian Church. In the chapter following the beautiful kenosis passage in Philippians 2, we see Paul expressing a similar humility but in and through his achievements, identity, and pursuit. Let's take a look at Paul's words on consecrated confidence in verses 2 through 14. He begins with a warning against the church of dogs, the evildoers, that are trying to get this church to put their confidence in things. These dogs add to the requirements for confidence. Even today, culture, outside and inside the Church (sadly), does the same. Expectations mixed with comparison can create a cocktail of confusing sources of confidence. But we are to boast only in Christ Jesus, nothing in the flesh. Paul then, to make a point against these dogs who were confusing this precious Church body, says a very unique statement: *"If someone else thinks they have reasons to put confidence in the flesh, I have more."* Paul is saying, "If you want to play that game, I will play too...I can play that game better than anyone I know."

Paul begins to unpack all the reasons he could be confident in the flesh, including his Jewish lineage. He could have put his trust in these things, but he did not. He could have put his trust and confidence in his list of accomplishments, degrees, family line, or other things. His list of achievements would make many other lists look a bit wimpy. He could walk around with swagger and confidence in most rooms...but once again, Paul provocatively flips it on its head.

Paul then declares that he is "a Hebrew of Hebrews" and as a Pharisee strictly followed the law, but he was not going to let tradition or morality be a source of his confidence. He calls all of that "garbage" (which is a tame translation). Paul looks at all of those things that could give one confidence in the flesh and lines it up with something substantially more impressive, sufficient, and unfailing for real confidence: Jesus.

Paul, in 1 Corinthians 2, speaks of this same power and confidence in Christ and Christ alone. These few verses speak of Paul's choice to only know Christ and Christ crucified as he addresses the Corinthian Church.

And so it was with me, brothers and sisters. When I came to you, I did not come with eloquence or human wisdom as I proclaimed to you the testimony about God. For I resolved to know nothing while I was with you except Jesus Christ and him crucified. I came to you in weakness with great fear and trembling. My message and my preaching were not with wise and persuasive words, but with a demonstration of the Spirit's power, so that your faith might not rest on human wisdom, but on God's power.

Paul chose to leave his Pharisee days behind, and even though he was a member of the tribe of Benjamin and had giftings in speaking, teaching, and leading, he focused on Christ and Him crucified. This not only redefined Paul's confidence, but it also realigned the Corinthian Church's confidence to rely on God's power when they were away from Paul.

The reality is that whatever you bring to the table for confidence will also be surpassed by Christ. All of those things are useless, a loss, compared to Christ and being found in Him. "Found in Him," being found in Christ, is essential for consecrated humble confidence. It is a freeing reality to know that we do not need to be exceptional, remarkable, or out of the ordinary. I have freedom to be unremarkable because I am found in Christ. *How about you?*

Christ's imputed righteousness = Christ's gift of confidence

Knowing Christ, being found in Him and receiving His righteousness, is the source of humble confidence. As grateful recipients, we can have plenty of achievements and sparkles or we can have very little . . . it just does not matter because Christ covers us in His righteousness. No longer can a dog or evildoer convince you that your confidence needs a little sprucing up or addition here or there. No, all that is garbage when it is compared to Jesus. When we feel like we need to do something to give us confidence, Paul starts talking about effort and striving but it's not in the people or things that we think of. He isn't talking about getting a degree, losing thirty pounds, or getting a new haircut. He starts using phrases like "press on," "take hold," and "straining toward what is ahead," not for the things that we think will give us confidence, but toward the things of Christ, the source of consecrated and humble confidence. Paul writes about suffering, death, and an upward heavenly call as the focuses of His pressing and straining. In the context of confidence, these are the things His eyes are fixed on. How about you?

You might read this and wonder, "So I stop working hard?" Redefining confidence does not redefine your calling. Calling and confidence are different things. I have a calling and I pursue what I need to accomplish it, but my confidence is not in how I achieve, perfect, or express my calling. That is obedience and abiding. My confidence must be in Christ, not my calling. We need high achievers but that is not where my brothers and sisters should find their confidence. Top-notch lawyers, doctors, actors, artists, and so on should be Christ followers so we can witness and love those who find themselves in those roles as well. As said in past chapters' conversations on celebrities, those who find themselves in roles that culture says are impressive probably will have greater temptations and hinderances to finding their confidence just in Christ, but I don't know...I am no doctor or businessman in a high-rise building. If we remember calling is a matter of obedience and abiding, and confidence is a matter of the cross and Christ, then we are in good shape.

A helpful practice or mindset that serves me in this

journey is the concept (which is imprinted on the front of my Bible) of "Grateful over gifted." It does not say "Grateful instead of gifted," nor does it say "Grateful I am gifted." It says "Grateful over gifted." This is a reminder that in all of your giftedness, just have gratitude outpace it. Be the most gifted preacher, parent, teacher, businessman, cop, or whatever... just always outpace your giftedness with gratitude for the very gift of Christ and of being found in Him. The reality is that all your giftedness, though you might have put in hours or sweat the sweat, is a gift from God anyway.

I think that might be a good start. I think this sort of gratitude is a good friend to consecrated humble confidence.

GRATEFUL

gifted

A PRACTICE FOR CONSECRATED HUMBLE CONFIDENCE

Many times, a different perspective or lens solves the problem. If we are tempted by something in our life that produces idolatry, unhealth, and pride, we want to pause and ask if we need to reorient and reengage in a different way. Reorienting how you steward does not always mean you have to relinquish them... but it may.

The following practice has aided me in chasing humble confidence. It helps me celebrate God's blessings and the unique gifts He's given me, and it purposefully places all of those things in the right spot in my heart, giving me biblical perspective. This practice can be done in a journal, scrap piece of paper, or even communally through intentional conversation. If you remember my doodle before about passing through the Throne Room...this is a practical way to walk that out.

1. Pray for the Spirit's leadership in this exercise.
2. Take inventory: Begin to list the elements in your life that you might gain confidence from. These can be skills or giftings, personality traits or knowledge, family or resources...list them.
   - One benefit of doing this in community, like between two friends, within a family, or a small group...it's a great time to encourage and call forth what you see in one another.
3. With your inventory of elements that give you confidence, walk through the following steps...

- **Contemplate**: Answer the following questions, or others, to help you gain insight.
  - *Who owns these things?*
  - *What's their purpose?*
  - *How can they be used for His glory and others' benefit?*
  - *What role do these serve in the Church?*
  - *Are any of these off-limits to Him? Why?*
- **Confession**—Confess how these things have been used for worldly confidence or ignored in self-reliance or self-deprecation.
- **Consecration**—Ask the Lord to help you engage with these things and show you how to steward and set them apart for His purposes.

- **Commission**—Pray that God would use all of these things for His Kingdom purposes and your formation, held in consecrated confidence. *If you are doing this with a partner or group, try praying over one another with the laying on of hands.*

Lord, help us look more like You and Your rooted confidence in who You are, whose You are, and what You were called to do. If any of these words distract, cause striving in the flesh, or just are not from You, help the reader toss them out. If any of these things are part of the readers' formation and were written by Your Spirit, thank You, and help them find fertile ground in their hearts to produce fruit for their lives and the Kingdom. Amen.

Chapter 7

Character

"The expression of Christian character is not in good but God-likeness. If the Spirit of God has transformed you within, you will exhibit Divine characteristics in your life, not good human characteristics. God's life in us expresses itself as God's life, not as human life trying to be godly."

OSWALD CHAMBERS

As a prisoner for the Lord, then, I urge you to live a life worthy of the calling you have received. Be completely humble and gentle; be patient, bearing with one another in love. Make every effort to keep the unity of the Spirit through the bond of peace.

EPHESIANS 4:1–3

Fifty to sixty thousand, a conservative guess, pilgrims descended on that two-stoplight town, the home to many students, faculty, and a few other Kentucky good ol' boys. The sweet town of Wilmore, Kentucky, feels like a mix of a Thomas Kincaid painting, a historic college town, and Jerusalem. It has an identity marked by many moves of God and an adorable downtown that hosts a Christmas event that rivals anything you'd watch on Hallmark. This city and its people, the staff of the two schools that call it home, and all the students attending the seminary and university would soon be bombarded by people from all over the world coming to experience God at the Asbury Outpouring. It is true that the city and institutions felt that weight of this moment in tremendous and indescribable ways. Traffic, plumbing, food, coffee, parking, and more were tested as God was moving, and so many wanted to experience it. There was a beautiful curiosity and hope. People deeply desire a move of God.

I don't believe anyone would say, "Naw, we don't want a divine encounter with the almighty God. We are good, stuffed to the brim. We'll catch it on the next round." We know and we pray for God to move in kindness and power in our midst. God was moving, and the people came. Some came to observe, curious or cynical, but others came and experienced the power of God. There was no audience and there were no performers. Only God's character was on display. Not an ethereal or conceptual version, but a tangible, living version that could be seen and heard. Christ's character, manifested by the Spirit or expressed by a brother or sister, kept on, saturating the space and the sixteen days.

Some of the sweetest moments of prayer for me happened in hallways and some of the most intense times of formation for me happened in meeting rooms and the cafeteria. One of the most corporate places of encounter, the place people rushed to at times, was the altar in Hughes Auditorium. This altar has history. For many years students have found themselves crying out, confessing, being strengthened, and waiting on the Lord at this altar.

Bud, a humble and heroic brother in Christ, and Jess, an administrative mastermind with a passion for encounter and awakening, quickly created a way to train ministers at the altar on leading prayer, deliverance, and other needed skills for what they'd encounter. This team would train 800 to 900 prayer ministers (remember, relatively spontaneously without planning) over the sixteen days. These trained volunteers would be given a lanyard that would give them the blessing to be at the altar and lead ministry there. This was our ragamuffin way of keeping the altar a place of purity and safety because those days got a little funky at times... that's for another book.

These dear teammates would sit at the altar for hours upon hours with a smile, anointing oil, a Bible, and a desire to partner with God. One day, I remember seeing the altar full of grown men who had driven all day and had just arrived after Hughes had been closed for cleaning and preparation for an evening service. We could not say no, and they did not pause or hesitate. They got to the altar and began to cry out. Another day, I saw Paul and Heather, good friends and local pastors, stand for almost nine hours at the altar with a line running up the aisle to the back door. Paul and Heather joyfully and confidently prayed, prayed, then prayed, then prayed some more at that altar. Dear friends from Pittsburgh drove to Wilmore and spent hours upon hours participating in ministry at the altar like cavalry coming over a hill for backup. My neighbors and their families were there every day, providing friendly faces and restful hugs for me but also a fierce focus on the freedom of those who found themselves at the front of Hughes.

The reality is that many folks, some who traveled miles and miles over oceans and many country lines, were underwhelmed with their first moments at Asbury. To some, it was confrontational and uncomfortable. Looking for loud, wow, sparkly, they experienced peace, simple and analog. It was not what they expected...but it was what was needed. Whether it was quick or came a little slower, Jesus' humility, kindness, and gentleness would move in their hearts. It felt extraordinarily ordinary with moments of silence, purposeful simplicity, and the gentleness of ministry at the altar or from the stage would collide with the loud, complex, and harsh reality that we often experience and have grown accustomed to. A little like Jesus, the moment we were experiencing was first underwhelming but quickly became overwhelming with His power and presence, like the disciples on the road of Emmaus.[1] At Asbury...

We were confronted with *humility*.

We had collided with *kindness*.

We were undone with *simplicity* and ministered to by *gentleness*.

Christ's character on display, our brokenness and desperation offered, and an Outpouring of encounter.

Not only was Christ's character on display supernaturally, vertically, but authentic Christ-like character was being expressed horizontally, in between one another. Pastors were kind and gracious to other pastors in their same part of town. The young were honoring the elder and the elder were stepping aside and championing the emerging generation with encouragement. People served one another, generosity was overflowing, and real humility was experienced in powerful ways through service, reconciliation, prioritizing the person next to you or in line over yourself, and in many more dazzling ways. Evangelistically, it felt almost like cutting butter with a warm knife...so many people had encountered the character of Christ and the Church in authentic Christ-likeness and humility that they could not wait to respond to the Gospel and give their lives to Jesus. Christ and His people witness to a watching world and the watching world were compelled to come to Christ...I will never forget this.

CHRISTIAN WITNESS

When I first gave my life to Christ, everyone spoke to me about my "witness." How I understood this concept was that drug usage, cursing, bursts of anger, freak dancing at homecoming, and other things were "bad witness." My immature understanding of witness was pretty much responding to adversity while not using colorful metaphors, not dabbling in illegal substances, and ultimately dancing more silly and less sexual were a "good witness." My simple mind just wanted to follow my new set of rules and I adopted this concept. I remember saying to myself "Worry about your witness"...that breaks down, doesn't it? An invitation to worry? (I am still going to counseling on this sort of stuff!)

This is a silly example of the concept of Christian witness, but there is a core truth nestled in my high schooler brain and spirit back then and in the understanding of the words about witness. It's much deeper and more impactful than "no more rap music and weed." When we have met Christ and given our lives over to Him, experiencing full forgiveness and relinquishing control of our lives, and are filled with the Spirit, our lives become a case for Christ. Our lives, our activity and character, is evidence of an encounter. Our witness, or the evidence of Christ's ownership of our lives and the filling and formation of the Spirit, becomes salt and light as Jesus' Sermon on the Mount describes. When we act like we have not met Christ and He does not own and operate our lives, nor does the Spirit have full control of our actions, we are not very effective evidence for the case of Christ. Now, this seems like a lot of pressure and in my brokenness, I have lived under this weight in unhealthy and non-Gospel-informed ways. We must remember that it's Christ in us, the Spirit's work through us, and that we lead from the lap of a gracious and unconditionally loving God. But we are a part of His family, and His family acts a certain way … just like how I was informing Eden, my oldest daughter, that Meerkreebses act a certain way when we are out to eat. Our faith is beautifully personal but not made to be private. Because of this, our character, formed by the Spirit and informed by Scripture, and the experience (evidence) of our life in and with Christ is possibly the best tool to introduce others to Jesus and live within Christian community.

This is why fighting for and prioritizing the formation of Christ-like character is so key. I am a fan, and student, of right doctrine, rich theology, and insightful Church history, but we cannot speak about right theology, sound doctrine, and biblical practices while negating and abandoning Christ-like character and the fruits of the Spirit. We cannot dissect Scripture or unpack systematic theology while negating love, joy, peace, patience, kindness, goodness, faithfulness, gentleness, and self-control. This work requires humility as the starting point. Without humility, we will pick and choose and hustle for character or we might express our knowledge and convictions like the world would and not like Jesus. His character is expressed through our uniqueness, personalities, and makeup like Psalm 139 beautifully highlights, but His character is the most captivating. This fight is against flesh and the enemy of our souls and for those we are in community with and those who have yet to meet or say yes to Jesus. C. S. Lewis masterfully and convincingly speaks to the submission and development of Christ-like character, powerful witness for Jesus, and the battle we fight in *The Screwtape Letters*. The letters in this wonderfully crafted and impactful book are fictional letters between demons that are strategizing how to take down a new believer, or their patient…

> Your patient has become humble; have you drawn his attention to the fact? All virtues are less formidable to us once the man is aware that he has them, but this is especially true of humility. Catch him at the moment when he is really poor in spirit and smuggle into his mind the gratifying reflection, "by Jove, I'm being humble," and almost immediately pride—pride in his own humility—will appear.[2]

The battle for and the formation of Christ-like character is no joke but when rooted in gritty, not-going-to-budge humility, we have hope. Saint Augustine expressed this sentiment when he stated that the top three virtues of Christianity are humility, humility, and humility. Humility is the foundation of

Christian character, like nutrient-rich soil that is ready for the seed of the Spirit to produce its fruit. In other words, humility of heart creates room for the Spirit to rule and reign and produce its fruit, which is Christ-likeness on display.

The gentleman who cuts my hair watches WWE reruns, loves a plethora of substances (some illegal), and is really curious about Jesus...not so much about the Church. Days after my daughter passed, I sat in his chair to get a haircut for Esther's funeral and I shared the Gospel with him. Every month or so, I pretty much do the same and often he responds with some of the most convicting words I hear these days...

"Jesus seems to be really kind, you'd think His people would be too."

"Zach, why are Christians so prideful and harsh when Jesus seemingly was different?"

"I would probably hang out with more Christians if they'd be cool with me."

Take your pulse and assess how you would respond. Maybe compassionately? Or did you start building a case for Christians? Did you start thinking about how Jesus was a little harsh at the temple or with Pharisees? Did you want to explain to my barber that kindness isn't the same as niceness, and since kindness can be misunderstood, we've got to stand our ground?

Theologically or scripturally, you and I may be able to run circles around my anime-loving and weed-smoking friend. But I wonder how Christ would respond and how His character might be on display as He sat in that chair and my barber shaved His beard or snipped His hair. I want to respond like Jesus, full of the fruits of the Spirit, and not like Zach might.

If our character is Christ-like, then our witness will be visible. During the time of the USSR, the KGB were looking for

Christians and churches, and do you know what they were instructed to look for? Kindness and generosity. It was assumed that the kindest and more generous people would ultimately lead them to an underground church because even the KGB knew that was how Christians, how Christ, would act. I wonder if we were in Soviet Russia or even in the early Church with Saul hunting us down what they would be advised to look for. Conservative posts on social media? Beautiful family portraits? Our bank statements and what we give to? Our Google calendars? Where our kids go to school? Or how we treat every single person we interact with?

CHRIST'S CHARACTER ON DISPLAY

In Bible times, Christ's incarnation and His interactions with every single person He met were opportunities to experience God's character incarnate. The characteristics that describe Him in Scripture put on flesh and expressed to all whom He is dwelling among. This confronted the religious, comforted the hurting, invited many to join in, and offered us a picture of character to long for. He was incarnate, with us, and when He was with us, we saw His kindness and humility on display!

In John 13 we get to join Jesus and His disciples in a significant moment after He arrives in Jerusalem on His way to the cross. This chapter is a tremendous microcosm of diverse, holy, and captivating characteristics of Jesus. Like watching a well-respected friend at a birthday party, observing how he or she acts and carries themself, we get to watch Jesus in such an intimate moment of ministry during His last meal with His disciples. In verse 3, his confidence and vision emerge. He knows who He is and what His Father had set for Him, then we see the beauty and very practical expression of Christ's servant heart and humility as He washes His disciples' feet. As the chapter continues, we see Christ as principled, focused, and bold. He speaks clearly to His disciples, teaching them and predicting His betrayal. In the final three verses, we see one of the most complex and captivating expressions of Christ's character when He speaks with graciousness and integrity while facing the disciple who betrays Him, Judas, and tells him to run his errand. Imagine this, someone has absolutely backstabbed you, betrayed you in such a way that will cost you greatly…even cost you your life. Those around the dinner table (or in the boardroom, or Zoom, or your church meeting) think this person might just be doing charity. You don't correct them, you don't slam this person with your words when the door closes behind him, you don't throw them under the bus, you allow your dinner guests to think kindly of your betrayer, your Judas. The other disciples don't realize what has happened and probably thought Jesus was telling Judas "to buy what was needed for the festival, or to give something to the poor" (John 13:29). Christ's character on display in the face of Judas and among His disciples: captivating and convicting.

Christ's character is on display throughout Scripture, in both the Old and New Testament, but in one unique passage, He shines a light on His very core…His heart. Dane Ortlund drills down and unpacks three verses that I believe are essential for the Christian to understand and might be one of the most evangelistically fruitful passages of our age. In his book, Ortlund writes,

In the one place in the Bible where the Son of God pulls back the veil and lets us peer way down into the core of who he is, we are not told that he is "austere and demanding in heart." We are not told that he is "exalted and dignified in heart." We are not even told that he is "joyful and generous in heart." Letting Jesus set the terms, his surprising claim is that he is "gentle and lowly in heart."[3]

This is not a fluffy reality to put in needlepoint or a sign in your living room but the very core of who Christ is. His humility and gentleness were on full display with who He chose to be to His disciples, whom He decided to share meals with, the women He championed in that cultural and historical context, and throughout His ministry. His gentleness with the woman caught in adultery is not flimsy and does not water down His holiness; it perfectly melds the two in Christ. His gentleness and lowliness as the discouraged and hopeless woman reached out and touched the hem of His garment, not running or being frustrated with her, is captivating. The blind beggar on the way to Jericho, the lepers, the tax collectors, the mourning sisters of His friend…humility and gentleness with skin on. Gentle and lowly had hands and feet, a mouth to express it, eyes to kindly look into their eyes, *your* eyes, and was not just written in a holy book. Christ's gentleness and humility walked the streets, traveled through towns, taught in temples, and belly laughed with friends. Christ's humility on display…all the way to the cross.

People can claim lots of things in writing. A dating app profile can list a number of characteristics that are shockingly incorrect on the first date. Résumés can be filled with fluff and lead to disappointment in the first interview or board meeting. Whether through dishonesty, a lack of self-awareness, or just shallow character…we can often be left wanting or disappointed. Jesus did not leave us wondering. The cross of Christ is such a stake in the ground and profound statement against that sort of disappointing or wishy-washy character. Someone could say all the things Christ did and never end up on the cross…proving them false and leaving us disappointed. But Jesus did not… Jesus got on the cross, proved His character, and showed us that all of what He taught and all He expressed is real. He is sacrificial and perfectly loving. He is humble and compassionate. Christ is dedicated and committed to you, to us, to the world. The cross was all of this on definitive display. His character, His glory, and His love collides with us through the cross. I will let you down…_____ will let you down… but the cross of Christ is a sign of Christ's faithfulness to you and that He is the same yesterday, today, and always.

Would you join me in resting in Christ's character today, right now, as you read these words? You don't need to wonder if He's real or just in a book; He is way better than you even imagined.

THE FRUITS OF THE SPIRIT: CHRIST-LIKE CHARACTER

I have met many men and women who have characteristics I aspire to. Dale and Louissa's generosity, Tasha's fierce protectiveness, Miriam's humor and wisdom, Ken and Christy's kindness, Ty's loyalty and commitment. I desire to look a little bit more like each one of those folks. I can aspire, prioritize, grit my teeth, and sometimes feel some shame that I just am not like those beautiful friends all the time. What about you? Do you ever see someone and appreciate their character and want to try hard, white-knuckling and hustling, to be a bit disappointed? The reality is that those are just elements of Christ's character that we are invited to experience. Christ is the better example. And good news—we do not have to try harder, fake it till we make it, or be driven by guilt when we act differently. Christ-like character can be cultivated, gifted to us, and then expressed through the fruits of the Spirit in us.

The fruits of the Spirit are described in Galatians, which is one of my favorite books in all of the Bible. It unpacks distinct ways of living, living in the Spirit, and living in flesh and law. Galatians 3:1–6 is a passage where we see sassy apostle Paul calling out this Church, the Church of Galatia, for forgetting that Christ has truly set them free. Their foolishness led to them forgetting that they are invited to live this life in the Spirit, through faith, and not in the flesh. This is a needed understanding for the development of Christ-like character. You will not get there through flesh and hard work. But we will experience the fruit through the Spirit. We have a wonderful invitation to ignore gritty imitation to embrace surrendered intimacy.

Humble intimacy with Jesus creates fertile soil for the Spirit to move and produce the fruits. Oh, and by the way, the Fruit (singular) of the Spirit *is not* the Fruits (plural…like a produce isle)…this matters. The Fruit of the Spirit is not an inventory to pick and choose from, prioritizing those easier for your personality or best fitting for that day. They are "*one*" fruit that we humbly submit to and watch the Spirit produce.

The Fruit of the Spirit, the character of Christ manifest in us through the Spirit, is in Galatians 5:22 and 23: the beauty of love, joy, peace, patience, kindness, gentleness, goodness, and self-control. These are nicknames for being Christ-like and are produced by the Spirit and not by you. Love without Jesus and the Spirit can be a form of passion or idolatry, leaving you disappointed or empty. Joy without the Spirit is just happiness on the outside and insincerity inside. Fake smiles and an Enneagram number are not a Fruit of the Spirit. Peace without the Spirit often looks like passivity or isolation, which is protection against anything uncomfortable or from something that might challenge us. Many things we pursue peace through offer temporary and flimsy peace. Often a certain personality type, gritting your teeth and shutting your mouth, or just polite behavior, can be perceived as patience, but without the Spirit, it's not patience. Kindness that is just niceness, often leading to hypocrisy, hiding, and self-protection, is not of the Spirit. Gentleness is a forgotten art of the Christian life. Remember, intensity and seriousness is not a fruit...gentleness is. And gentleness without the Spirit can quickly lead to coddling, codependency, losing self and agency. Gentleness is often misunderstood like humility, leading to passivity and sitting back. Follow Jesus' example of gentleness and you will learn differently.

Do you want a life of self-righteousness, limited morality, and behavior modification? Or true goodness? You'll need the Fruit of the Spirit if you want real goodness and not those disheartening lesser things. Self-help, strategic alarms, productivity apps, rule, and religion are not fruits of the Spirit, *but* self-control is. Self-control is not constricting and subduing... it is freedom with Christ and fueled by the Spirit. So, like Paul in Galatians, I wonder if you want to live your life, express your character, living by the law and flesh or by the Spirit. This Spirit was received by faith and faith alone, not by being nice and extra-Christian.

The distinct differences between these characteristics in the Spirit versus in the flesh is not just semantics. I believe it's life and death, or at least living or dying. Christ promises us life and life everlasting. When we are striving in self-help behavior modification and looking Christian, we ultimately are putting plastic play fruit on a living organic tree. It's silly. But we do it often. Jesus invites us to do the patient and precious work of life in the Spirit producing real fruit. Behaving Christian and befriending Christ are very different. Befriending the Spirit of God and allowing it to work in your life, producing these attributes, is life-giving and freeing. I've lived too much of my life behaving and not befriending and I hope you would, like me, throw in the towel and quit that and pursue friendship with Jesus. Within the context of the beautiful passage of abiding (friendship with Jesus), we see the truth of John 15:15, "*I no longer call you servants, because a servant does not know his master's business. Instead, I have called you friends, for everything that I learned from my Father I have made known to you.*" Does your growth and maturing of Christ-likeness feel like slavery and servanthood or the result of sweet friendship with Jesus? One way you can assess this is when you don't act like one of the Fruits of the Spirit or like Jesus...how do you respond and where do you run off to? Into shame and hiding, afraid of a "master," or colliding with the grace and hope of friendship with Jesus?

I am currently learning this in brand-new, and convicting, ways. In most Christian contexts, I don't seem religious. It's funny because people assume I'm not because I have tattoos and wear Birkenstocks most days. I usually have a beard and I really like Will Farrell movies (I don't know if I should write that in a Christian book). But it turns out you can have tattoos, wear Birkenstocks, and watch Will Farrell and still struggle with being religious. In this last year, following the unique outpouring at Asbury, I have been in the continual work of confrontation, crucible, and crushing. Most of this work is around my unrealistic expectations of self, religious standards I hold myself to, and the fear of messing up. This is not life in the shadow of the cross and all it offers; it's a life of religion. I don't struggle with this always, but I want to be honest, as I have been throughout each sentence of this book, that I can struggle with this. I think many people do. Possibly not with the big hairy things we know we should stay away from in our Christian walk, but the intimate and personal places of our journey. Kindness slips into Christian niceness or humility disappears into prideful false humility to save face. Not specifically on purpose but often because we really want to be kind and humble and we try hard, try hard, try harder, and forget that we got here through faith, the cross, and the Spirit producing those things in our lives. We fall into a life of behaving Christian instead of befriending Christ. We miss it. Sad to say, often I miss it.

Jesus, gentle and kind, is fierce for this sort of freedom and Fruit of the Spirit. He rebukes the religious for cleaning the outside of the cup and not the inside. I don't often feel like a Pharisee, but this passionate and fierce rebuke, seen in Matthew 23, is saturated with Christ's commitment to the freedom He offered. Religion doesn't offer freedom but rather leads us to gritting teeth and white-knuckling instead of resting in Christ and seeing the Fruit produced by the Spirit. When I gave my life to the Lord at age sixteen, I replaced one standard and moral compass (or lack thereof) with Christian morals. Instead of prioritizing transformation through abiding, in many ways I prioritized hard work and behavior modification.

We must remember that all of this development of Christ-likeness is a result of the cross and nothing else. Without the cross, we aren't adopted. Without Jesus' death, we don't get the Spirit to regenerate in us, leading us to becoming the new man or woman we're made to be. If we did not receive Christ's justifying work, no sort of character development could do the trick. We would just be nice and polite, without hope. The more we rest as children of God, coheirs with Christ, and recipients of the Spirit, we will see godly character emerge and that will compel the world to pay attention to the message we have.

A PRACTICE FOR EXPLORING AND EXPRESSING CHRIST-LIKE CHARACTER

When I meet someone I admire, I like to learn how they express those things I admire. Follow me here...when you watch a fellow student do well in classes, aren't you curious to know their study practices? When you watch a married couple handle stress and conflict really well, don't you want to observe their ways of communication and being a team? We do this when we follow someone on social media who expresses their faith in a captivating way or has lost weight in a way that seems manageable for you, or when we ask to be mentored by someone more successful in our vocation, or we take classes from experts. This is not rocket science.

One practice I've adopted and would love to invite you into is doing the same, somewhat plainly and casually, with Jesus. I often am "studying" a book of the Bible more in depth during my times with the Lord, but each time I have my Bible open, I finish with a period of time just watching Jesus through the Gospel. I don't study the Greek, cross-reference, ask all sorts of formational questions...I just watch. I watch how He reacts, how He serves, how He teaches and corrects. I set an alarm, sometimes five minutes and sometimes more, and literally just ask one question...

"What does it reveal about His character?"

Knowing Christ's character does not immediately mean you've adopted and express Christ-like character but it does give you new ways to pray and examples to follow. So would you do the same? As you open up God's Word, continue in your normal practices and rhythms, but finish your time, possibly five to ten minutes, watching Jesus and asking that simple question: "What does it reveal about His character?" Here is an example...

- Read Mark 5.
- What does it reveal about Christ's character?
- I would just make a list in my journal...here are some things that stuck out to me...
  - *Fearless*
  - *Confident*
  - *Knows His authority*
  - *Hospitable to anyone*
  - *Willing and respectful*
  - *Principled*
  - *Compassionate*

- ○ *Available and accessible*
- ○ *Not shaming, empathetic and curious*
- ○ *Focused*
- ○ *Gentle and kind*
- Then I would contemplate throughout the day about these characteristics and pray for me to grow in these areas as well.

———————————

Lord, I don't want to seem Christian. I want to resemble Christ. Thank You for the Fruit of the Spirit. We long for greater expression of those Fruits, not for our own gain but for a witness to draw others to You.

God, thank You for the Outpouring and the opportunity to write on these things. If any of these words or ideas are not of You and not helpful for the reader's growth with You, help them forget it! BUT if any of these things are of You and would advance their formation and the Kingdom, may it be so! Amen.

section three

The Potential of Humility

Chapter 8

Compelling

"To get even near humility, even for a moment,
is like a drink of cold water to a man in a desert."

C. S. LEWIS

"There's nothing more relaxing than humility."

TIMOTHY KELLER

"Humble yourselves before the Lord,
and he will lift you up."

JAMES 4:10

Someone texted me while I was in class and I could not get here sooner!"

"I saw it on socials and had to come!"

"We filled a couple vans and got here as quick as we could!"

"We sold our car to buy tickets to come worship with you all here."

"I drove thirty-five hours to get here, with my two boys... we needed this."

"We were about to board the plane but heard about Asbury in the airport and changed our tickets."

What was so compelling about what God was doing at Asbury for those sixteen days? We saw, conservatively, fifty to sixty thousand people come from all over the world to experience God. It was not because of the preaching, the worship artist, or the innovative programming and style. It was not convenient to get to like a major metropolitan center nor was it roomy with lots of space to host comfortably. Asbury had not cracked the code on registrations and marketing nor had we planned for months or years. All the things that normally capture our eyes and compel our hearts did not show up, no, but God did... in power like I've never experienced.

Early in the Asbury Outpouring, I opened up Scripture to facilitate a time of the public reading of God's Word. I felt led, as I did multiple times following, to read portions of Isaiah 55, an invitation for the thirsty...

> *"Come, all you who are thirsty,*
> *come to the waters;*
> *and you who have no money,*

come, buy and eat!
Come, buy wine and milk
without money and without cost.

Why spend money on what is not bread,
and your labor on what does not satisfy?
Listen, listen to me, and eat what is good,
and you will delight in the richest of fare.

Give ear and come to me;
listen, that you may live.
I will make an everlasting covenant with you,
my faithful love promised to David.

See, I have made him a witness to the peoples,
a ruler and commander of the peoples.

Surely you will summon nations you know not,
and nations you do not know will come running to you,
because of the LORD your God,
the Holy One of Israel,
for he has endowed you with splendor."

The hungry and thirsty came and they delighted in the richest of fare. Nations we did not know came running, hearing from God through social media and word of mouth. God had come down and endowed us with the splendor of His peaceful presence. Memories of the line wrapping around campus, leaving some folks waiting for eight or nine hours, is wild to me, and those who came from all over the world to come worship with us was quite humbling. What was God doing? What was happening? I think we are still trying to figure this out.

Revivalists and skeptics alike found themselves encouraged and challenged by what they saw. I sat with individuals who have devoted their life to studying and contending for revival in their lifetime. I think they were relatively surprised, maybe dissatisfied, when I really did not know anything about the historical moments they were talking about. Multiple times, I was given, in person or left in my makeshift office, a printout of a PhD dissertation about "revival." Megachurch pastors, worship artists, and influential Christian leaders came and sat, soaking in Christ's presence and peace. The diversity of the audience was beautiful and a picture of the Church. Along with Christian leaders, revivalists, and pastors, we had Wiccans, brothers and sisters without homes, drug dealers, and we even met a man who was released from jail an hour or so earlier and immediately got a ride to Asbury. The light of Christ radiated out and like a lighthouse in a harbor, ushered in sojourners from all over the world...it did not matter who you were, where you came from, or what you brought.

About halfway through those two weeks in Hughes Auditorium and the surrounding churches and campus, my friend and his wife brought a young woman into the chapel I had been praying for over many years. My friends have a powerful ministry of deliverance and freedom that has impacted many people, including myself. Their guest had never been able to sit in worship because of a terrible childhood in which she was groomed by a satanic cult. She had seen and experienced such dark things over the years and was so heavy with despair and spiritual darkness. My dear friends served her with hospitality, prayer, and care and asked if she would join them in

Hughes. To their surprise, she came...she had never been able to say the name of Jesus out loud without a violent response. We all wondered how this would go...shame on us, God was on the move and His eyes were on this sweet girl. This young woman sat, still and stoic in her seat. An hour went by and then another. About two hours later, this young woman peacefully and quietly leaned over and whispered the name above every other name, a name she had not been able to mutter: "Jesus."

Over the day, she said Jesus' name louder and louder like waves of piercing peace and freedom, and by the evening she looked visibly different and was standing, with her hands raised, worshipping the one who had come in power and peace for her that day...Jesus. No profound prayer, or deliverance ministry, or preaching to cast something out. The peace and kindness of Christ confronted the despair, harshness, hatred, and hurt she was steeped in from a young age. She had met the humble King and He cared for her.

Since the Outpouring, this young woman has changed her name and is attending a local church with my friends. Jesus is compelling. Often we get in the way, like standing in front of a beacon and blocking its vibrant hope and power with ourselves.

COUNTERCULTURAL

I believe one of the most compelling things about Jesus is how humbly countercultural He was in His day and age. We often think of being countercultural as prideful, provocative, and overall prideful and spicy. But like how Christ's humility confronts us (check back on chapter two), our humility can be countercultural now. Could you imagine how compelling

the Church, operating countercultural to pride and position-
ing, would be to those we love and desire to know and experience Jesus if our communities were known by our humility?
How might radical humility confront the pride and selfishness
all over the world, experienced in life and seen all over social
media, and compel the world to explore the very source and
perfect example of that humility? How might humility shine
a light on the brokenness of secularism and other worldviews
and invite them to meet our humble King? Could Christ be
compelling the world with His radical humility...through His
people? I pray that we would be ready and willing to be marked
by humility and stay countercultural to a narrative saturated
with pride and self. Andrew Murray, in his book *Humility*,
casts this compelling and sobering vision of humility in need
of strong faith:

> If humility is Christ's greatest virtue, is it any wonder
> that the Christian life is so often weak and fruitless,
> when the very root of Christian life is neglected and
> unknown...Until humility that rests in nothing less
> than the end and death of self, and which gives up all
> honor of men as Jesus did to seek the honor that comes
> from God alone that God may be all, that the Lord
> alone may be exalted—until such a humility is what we
> seek in Christ above our chief joy, and welcome at any
> price, *there is very little hope of faith that will conquer
> the world.*[1]

We do not need much convincing that the world needs
something more. As Christians, we believe it is Christ. Christ
is the answer. But is the Christ message we are sharing the

fullness of who He really is and experienced or are we painting a picture with just our favorite and possibly most comfortable colors, often omitting potentially one of its most vibrant "colors," humility?

The American Church can struggle with weakness, suffering, fragility, and...humility. Humility confronts the American dream that has sadly seeped into our churches. Prior to the Outpouring, I did not use my platform or voice to tell the story of Christ's radical humility, freeing fragility, and the centrality of suffering in our Christian walk. However, after seasons of struggle and the loss of our daughter, I repented to Jesus and to many I had invested in. I have confessed that "Pastor Zach" of pre-Covid would've not known what to do with present Zach.

Today, I am messier, but probably more honest, and I experience Christ's closeness more than ever. When I look at many young men and women that I had the gift of shepherding in college and youth ministry, I sometimes grieve that I did not create more space to experience Christ's lowliness and gentleness. Many times, saturated with charisma and passion, I preached messages that did not include, or even sometimes scoffed at, messages about radical humility, meekness, and the gift of obscurity and slowness. We must exhort but also teach a countercultural humility that we hope to steward well.

If we desire to be compelling, all of what we need is in Jesus. We don't have to spin it or spice it up...He is sufficiently countercultural. To compete with the leading business and leadership voices that have the same message, except with a flavored Jesus, seems silly. Jesus did not mirror Caeser except with kinder words and a more well-behaved life. Christ flipped it all on its head with His radical humility and gentleness. This is compelling not because it's provocative but because it's powerful. Christ's message and humility is power, not puny. Christ's humility is an assault on the world and its practices, not an acquiescence. We see this throughout Scripture as we watch Christ's life on full display through the Gospels, possibly in the most compelling ways in His final days on earth. Christ's humility in the Garden of Gethsemane, praying to His Father and waiting for His betrayer instead of strategizing and getting out of Dodge exudes humble character. Jesus was silent and singularly focused, fully submitted in humility to the Father, through His arrest, judgment, and trial. Christ calling Judas "friend" and rebuking Peter for cutting the slave's ear off both exude Christ's character at this crucible moment.

In his most countercultural moments, Jesus stood before Pilate and the crowd called for a murderous robber to be freed. Christ did not flex His power and glory, knocking everyone to the ground and into their senses. He knew to be silent while on His way to the cross for our behalf. Christ's humility was countercultural and confusing to Pilate and concerning to Pilate's wife. As Christ hung on the cross, he remained humble as onlookers and soldiers hurled insults and teased him. Christ even ministered to the robber next to him and enjoyed his presence later in paradise. In these moments when Christ would be the most likely to leak pride or exude supernatural, self-protecting strength ... He stayed humble and engaged with the criminal next to Him, and He forgave those who put Him through misery. In fact, He went lower. Descending in humility leading to lifting up, *Christ takes His most humble steps right before His most glorious ones*. Naked, tattered, spat on, and killed right before robes, healed, crowned, and resurrected in glory. This countercultural humility and ministry to you and me is beautifully explained by Keller in his book on suffering,

Jesus lost all his glory so that we could be clothed in it. He was shut out so we could get access. He was bound, nailed, so that we could be free. He was cast out so we could approach. And Jesus took away the only kind of suffering that can really destroy you: that is being cast away from God. He took so that now all suffering that comes into your life will only make you great. A lump of coal under pressure becomes a diamond. And the suffering of a person in Christ only turns you into somebody gorgeous.[2]

This is compelling humility. This is Christian humility radiating from our Jesus. This humility is the only way we could be saved. Thank you, Jesus, for your humility on the cross!

EXPRESSING HUMILITY

Humility draws curiosity. And humility pushes past curiosity and compels people to Christ. In the Book of Acts, we see the early Church living in the reality of compelling humility and the characteristics that flow from it. The disciples waited in humility for the Spirit to come, and empowered by the Spirit, not their zeal or competency, Peter stepped forward and preached. As the Church began, it was saturated with humility with reliance on the apostles' teaching, radical generosity, hospitality, and inclusivity. In Acts 4, those coming against them even commented on their humble nature: *"When they saw the courage of Peter and John and realized that they were unschooled, ordinary men, they were astonished and they took note that these men had been with Jesus"* (Acts 4:13). In humility, Christ's followers delegated and empowered deacons, in humility Stephen was martyred while praying for his killers, in humility Ananias went and in humility Saul responded. In humility Barnabas vouched for Paul and in humility the Antioch Church sent them out. Humility was expressed beautifully in the early Church because they had lived so closely to capital *H* Humble in the flesh, Jesus, and walked in His ways.

Like the early Church, humility applied to key areas of our life creates compelling characteristics that are a gift to those brothers and sisters in Christ and impactful to those who do not know Him yet. Humility is a salt and light characteristic. Humility permeates the beatitudes and expresses itself, through you, as salt and light to a world in need of Jesus. They notice your lowliness and kindness and you point them to Jesus. This sort of humility is a resistance to what the world says, just like the beginning of the Sermon on the Mount depicts. Pursuing humility is rebellion to a world ruled by pride, striving, and gathering to gain. Rich Villodas writes, "Humility—like poverty of spirit in the beatitudes—is the way to true freedom. The person marked by humility has nothing to prove, nothing to possess, and nothing to protect. This is true freedom."[3] This sort of freedom is expressed in the life of the Church and the disciple in multiple compelling ways, including the following.

Leadership—leadership marked by Christ-like humility is both captivating and controversial. Conferences, books, podcasts, and coaching are all available to help the leader grow and succeed. The number of resources for leadership and the plethora of convictions around it communicate the importance of leadership itself. Romans 12 speaks of the gift of leadership and charges those given it to lead with all due diligence and 1 Corinthians 12 speaks of a multitude of gifts also present in the Church. First Thessalonians speaks to the reader and instructs them to respect those leading over them. Jesus, by example and correction, looks at the leadership around Him and gives us a new template. This template is exemplified in the repeated passage through this book, Philippians 2:5–11. Jesus in perfect humble leadership did not cling and flex His platform, title, or rights but released them for the sake of others. When compelling humility is applied to practical leadership, we will see a self-emptying (kenotic) leader. A servant leader who raises up those around them without offense or corruption of character.

The most flesh-burning and humbling leadership role I have ever experienced were the sixteen days at Asbury. We spoke about a nameless and faceless movement of the Spirit, and leaders committed to Romans 12 love and Philippians 2 posture. It was all tested, and the reality is, your humble leadership will be too. Choosing to hold no offense requires humility. This sort of humble leadership excels when Jesus and His mission are in the driver's seat and not our own motives and preferences.

A round table with Jesus in the middle, facilitated and stewarded by a team or selected leader, can lead to the expression of each teammate's vibrancy and gifting without subduing and cancelling out the other. This sort of humble leadership has been called *mutually submissive leadership, polycentric leadership*, or simply *team leadership*. Imagine a toddler's watercolor painting. It begins with distinct and separate colors, like a Crayola watercolor set. After they have soaked the watercolors and painted on their paper, the picture often resembles mud with a tint of the child's favorite color.

When my Eden would paint, it was usually pretty hard to distinguish the colors on the page, but it was often tinted her favorite colors, pink or purple. This is how many teams work, believing the lie that humility is subduing oneself and sitting back, which leads to muddiness and just submitting to the loudest voice or most convincing person's "favorite color." Now compare this to a vibrant stained-glass window. Vibrancy can hold its place next to another being vibrant and humble, like a stained-glass window. In fact, color theory shows us that all colors have complementary colors that actually bring out the brilliance of both colors next to each other. The stained glass is distinct, diverse, but all together for a common purpose...in this example, to project or resemble an image. In humble Christian leadership,

distinct and diverse leaders are placed together for the common goal to portray Christ through their selected vision, mission, and values. This is not only requiring the individual to pursue humility but the team in itself. With a humble facilitator of vision and mission, the team can step forward in their "lanes" and humbly follow and accomplish their vision.

Self-Awareness—Self-awareness might be one of the most underrated characteristics out there. A self-aware disciple is one that stays low and dependent. The ability to know oneself, one's shadows and strengths, creates fertile ground for sobriety and humility and prepares someone well to avoid the seduction of pride. When you know God and all He has done for you, it's hard to be prideful. When you really know yourself and your needs and slip-ups, it's hard to be prideful as well. Knowing oneself is at the center of Christian salvation. You must acknowledge who you are without Jesus and who He is for you…the Savior and your King. Without this sobriety, we won't find ourselves resting in Jesus.

I believe the continual success and ebbs and flows of personality tests, even BuzzFeed quizzes, support this longing to know oneself. Myers-Briggs helping one realize how they take in information, SDI revealing how we deal with adversity, StrengthsFinders affirming our superpowers, and Enneagram reading our minds and telling us our true intentions…these all scratch an itch to know oneself. They aren't evil, though they can be idolized and elevated over Christ's voice, which is not good, but they are tools to help us realize our strengths and weaknesses. If these tools, among many others, are stewarded well, we experience deeper freedom in humility by knowing who we are and our need for God. Self-awareness offers tremendous clarity in our formation journey. When self-awareness is wielded correctly, it leads to compelling humility and permission for individuals to be themselves.

Joy—C. S. Lewis has many compelling insights on humility, one of them being:

"Do not imagine that if you meet a really humble man, he will be what most people call 'humble' nowadays: He will not be a sort of greasy, smarmy person who is always telling you that, of course, he is nobody. Probably all you will think about him is that he seemed a cheerful, intelligent chap who took a real interest in what you said to him. If you do dislike him it will be because you feel a little envious of anyone who seems to enjoy life so easily. He will not be thinking about humility; he will not be thinking about himself at all."[4]

A humble person is marked by joy (remember the last chapter about the Fruit of the Spirit?). That joy is not cheap happiness, because the humble person is authentic and honest and in no need of faking it, but a joy rooted in knowing who they are and who God is. This assessment, wrapped up in gratitude and set down into the rich soil of humility, will produce joy in such a compelling way. Like Lewis said, it might even be confrontational and annoying. Have you ever met someone like that? With joy rooted in healthy humility that kind of confronts your striving and performance-based assessments?

We live in a world that is saturated with sadness, and the government recently stated that we are in a "loneliness epidemic." Humble joy is a sweet balm to this reality. Humility helps us suffer well with rooted joy. Humility serves those toiling, doing hard work, with joy and gratitude. Joy sprouting from humility might be the very door that many meet Jesus at in this coming generation. Humility-produced joy is like the perfect tomato at the farmer's market or the most beautiful flower at the nursery…it comes from the right source, has been nurtured with the right stuff, and will bless the one who takes it home. Compelling joy flowing from Christian humility, develop this in us, Lord!

Rest—We are the salt and light of the earth and we get to rest in this day and age. In this moment, especially where I am sitting and serving, the people are tired, busy, and quite exhausted. When Christians understand their standing because of the cross, they can truly rest. Humble rest, not prideful laziness, is compelling to a weary world. Of course, a beautiful resort vacation or bougie cruise is compelling…but not in the way that a truly humble disciple is at rest in their soul. We find this through humble acceptance of Jesus as the true Sabbath (Hebrews 4).

We are not talking about compelling the world by being "chill" or relaxed. We are talking about being free of striving, competition, and comparison. In high school, I loved soccer though I was not great. Every year, our high school team would dye their hair pink (I think it was trying to be red) for the play-offs, which was a tradition for the team because they often won the state championship. My junior year, they were kind enough to let me dye my hair…as a friend…I was not on the team. That year they won state and "hey-oh!" I had matching hair.

The week following their big win, I walked into soccer tryouts and a coach kindly interrupted me getting ready and told me I did not need to try out and that they'd call me later. They must have heard I was not that good…bummer…I drove home. To my surprise I got a call telling me I got invited to one of the top teams and a congratulations for winning state. They had no clue I did not play; they just knew I had pink hair and assumed. When we are in Christ, our tryouts are cancelled, and we can rest. There is no more striving or winning our spot on the team. Because of the cross and our acceptance, we are in. Just like with my pink hair, I could rest. In our humble acceptance and life with Christ, we don't have to keep trying out…we got pink hair and we don't care. This sort of rest is compelling to a tired world. This sort of rest only comes from the work on the cross, the invitation of Jesus, and our humility to accept.

Humility is not to be just held on to for yourself but expressed for those who need to meet Jesus. "*Let your light so shine before men, that they may see your good works, and glorify your Father which is in heaven*" (Matthew 5:16, KJV). Christ-like humility is some of that light.

COMPELLING GEN Z

As God poured out on Asbury's campus, a generation that many have written off led the way. According to many researchers and experts, Generation Z, those approximately eleven through twenty-six years of age, is experiencing a great exodus from the Church and they're dissolving into culture and all it brings. At the Outpouring, I saw something different. I now know a different story. Christ came and compelled Gen Z with something real and authentic, the very thing they've been begging for.

Through Asbury students the news spread, first to their peers and then beyond. They were simply invited to stay to experience God's love so that they could authentically love others, and a handful stayed but soon many others were compelled to come back. I will never forget seeing students that I coach and have prayed for for years poking their heads through the doors to check out what was going on. Many students that I love and have yet to meet Jesus were in the front rows engaging in different ways for a majority of those days and one of my beloved friends, a Muslim student at Asbury, was in a random seat throughout the chapel most days…just watching. Encountering Jesus is compelling.

Gen Z was encountering Jesus in such a way that they were captivated. Not only captivated and encouraged, they were experiencing healing. Generation Z experienced healing by meeting the head of the Church, Jesus, and experiencing His captivating character. So many of the emerging generation have experienced the Church displaying characteristics that are off-putting and unlike Jesus. It feels fake and inauthentic. Insecure and striving while being harsh and unforgiving. It seems like spiritual catfishing, promising and promoting one thing and showing up differently. It is deflating and it leaves them longing for Jesus and leaving His Church.

Dr. Kevin Brown, president of Asbury University and a dear friend and teammate in the trenches of the Outpouring, tells a story of a student correcting him as they were debriefing the sixteen days. This student said, "No, we don't want something more…we want something less." When the world, or the Church, tells us we need more stuff, more skill, more to capture their attention, more posts, whatever, we might listen to this young man and his desire for less. This is so compelling to me; what about you? Yes, it is complicated and can be unpacked, of course, but meeting Christ and experiencing His characteristics, both supernaturally and relationally with others, warmed their hearts. All generations, experiencing Christ in fullness, regained hope…not in Asbury or how we stewarded the sixteen days but in Jesus and His Church!

This generation wants authentic and honest, real healing experiences after hearing, reading about, or even experiencing dishonest or cocky Christian leaders and flimsy and fragile church communities. Dr. Brown says, "Students are less interested in 'beliefs' than in a faith that works. There is a trenchant meaning vacuum in our country fostering a sweeping spiritual hunger." During those sixteen days, we hosted visitors from approximately 285 colleges or universities and many Gen Z led, not volunteered but led, in key areas of the Outpouring. Their hunger was colliding with honest and humble Jesus. The phrases "Nameless and Faceless" and "the only celebrity here is Jesus" refreshed their weary souls and social media feeds. The gentleness and kindness of Jesus was oozing from Hughes Auditorium, into the lawn, the line, and the other simulcast venues. They were hungry for humble and honest, and they were being fed. This did not just happen on Asbury's campus but many other campuses full of Gen Z men and women like Baylor, University of Michigan, Texas A&M, Cedarville, Lee University, Samford University, and Auburn. Recently, almost a year following the Outpouring at Asbury, approximately fifty-five thousand Gen Z men and women gathered in Mercedes-Benz Stadium for the Passion conference and sought the Lord together through worship and teaching. They encountered the Spirit of God in such a powerful way that some people are referring to it as "That moment at Passion." Gen Z has been compelled, and honestly now, Gen Z is compelling us, the world.

This generation is compellingly extreme and does not mince words. More and more, if this generation has a vibrant walk with Jesus, they've counted the cost in some way. Gen Z is pursuing spirituality but rejects fluff and wants real. I have never seen this much curiosity and hunger about the things of Jesus. Though they desire authentic spirituality, they are still not coming back to church. Why is that? They want action and they want honesty. Covid, occurring during many of Gen Z's formational years, almost secularized Sundays and scattered spiritual encounters to YouTube videos, social media posts, and small gatherings. There is an answer, but would we include our Gen Z brothers and sisters, our sons and daughters maybe, in the discussion about the solution? Their hunger reminds me of a young emerging leader we read about in Scripture. If this young leader has any prophetic impact on the outcome and direction Gen Z is going, we will be all right. This young leader, probably the age of many of our Gen Z friends, was following the beloved Moses.

In his old age, Moses would gather his things for the tent of meeting and head out of town to set it up. The Israelites would stand at the mouths of their own tents to watch what would happen next. Moses would set up the tent and the pillar of cloud would descend on the entrance and everyone would watch. This story in Exodus 33:7–11 feels a bit like those sixteen days at Asbury. A tent of meeting a bit out of town (through horse farms) and when the presence of God came, it seemed like everyone noticed and watched. Not only would the onlookers watch, but they would worship…like many of our brothers and sisters did around the world whether through a live feed, YouTube video, or thirty-two-second Instagram reel. The world, this generation, was compelled because God's presence fell. In the tent of meeting, radical intimacy occurred as it is said, "The Lord would speak to Moses face-to-face, as one speaks to a friend." What feels significant and parallel to our story is what comes next, after the established leader and older generation returned to camp: "His servant Joshua, the son of Nun, a young man, would not leave the tent." Joshua, the emerging leader, was so compelled by the friendship, encounter, and presence of God that he was not going to run back to camp but linger, hungry for more. This is what we saw and this is what we long for. As my friend contending for renewal and leading movement in the UK prays, "Lord, raise up a generation that does not want to leave the tent." We saw many compelled to come, lingering and longing for more, and now they are compelling us to not move on too fast but pick humility and hunger and contend for more.

TEARING DOWN HIGH PLACES

In the Book of Judges, among other books of the Old Testament, there are heart-wrenching lists of leaders who "did what they thought was right" and did not follow the Lord. Almost always it seemed that this was rooted in pride and the people were the victims of their king's arrogance. Idol worship, sexual brokenness, terrible violence, and failure on the battlefield were the consequence of prideful and disobedient leaders. There was a vacuum of holy and humble leadership. But once in a while, there would be a humble king who would do what was right in the eyes of the Lord. In 2 Kings 18, we read about a twenty-five-year-old leader (shout-out Gen-Z) that stepped up and led with consecrated confidence. Second Kings 18:3–6 speaks of some of his first steps of leadership,

> *He did what was right in the eyes of the LORD, just as his father David had done. He removed the high places, smashed the sacred stones and cut down the Asherah poles. He broke into pieces the bronze snake Moses had made, for up to that time the Israelites had been burning incense to it. (It was called Nehushtan.)*
>
> *Hezekiah trusted in the LORD, the God of Israel. There was no one like him among all the kings of Judah, either before him or after him. He held fast to the LORD and did not stop following him; he kept the commands the LORD had given Moses.*

Hezekiah, a young man, tore down the high places. The people had once understood that God met them on high and secluded places, but now those same sacred spaces were perverted into places of idol worship. These intermingled places of glory and idolatry were the first things in Hezekiah's crosshairs. There would be no more spiritual casualness or selfish pride. One of the most *compelling* aspects of humility is that we continue to seek the Lord and follow His Word in each season of our life. A humble leader understands this key kingdom principle: In the world we mature out of need, but in the Kingdom, we mature into need.

This twenty-five-year-old king knew he could not keep the status quo and recognized he was desperate to humbly trust the Lord and obey in a new way. Hezekiah's zeal and leadership shines bright. I wonder if we might need to go and examine our own high places and purify their purposes and priorities. Might there be something that you need to tear down or just press "restart" and refocus? I have watched churches and chapels reorient their entire rooms as (the Spirit) convicted them that the stage and LED lights distracted because they had become more of a temptation to pride than an invitation to preach the Gospel in boldness and humility. I have seen families change schools or move, businesses reorient org-charts and titles, tight schedules being stretched to linger, and more. Social media accounts, publishing, conferences, and other elements are being examined and being reoriented. What are the high places in your life? Have they become intermingled with idolatry or self?

Lord, help us be like Hezekiah … zealous and bold …
in tearing down the high places.

As he tore down the high places, Hezekiah also went and examined how once a good thing, the Asherah pole made by Moses,[5] had been distorted and became an idol. In the Book of Numbers 21 the Israelites became impatient and began to complain. The Lord sent snakes to discipline the people, but through Moses' prayerful plea, God gave him some strange instructions. The Lord said to Moses, "Make a snake and put it up on a pole; anyone who is bitten can look at it and live."[6] There would have been stories about this. There would have been expectations. But over time there was also corruption. Pause and think this through: This young king was courageous enough to destroy the thing that once offered his people supernatural healing from God. An old thing became a broken thing that led the king to move to do a new thing. When a good thing ceases to be a God thing, you get rid of it. This is compelling consecrated confidence. Maybe it's time to examine an old thing that has become an idol, a golden heifer, that really just needs to be destroyed. We often idolize good things like leaders, resources, education, family, or even forms of worship. We need to humbly address those things.

God, help us humbly rely on Your every word
and take courageous steps to smash idols.

As you follow King Hezekiah's story through the next two chapters, you will see that the king's humility was not only compelling to his people but to God. First, Hezekiah was threatened by the Assyrians, who were terrible and scary. Hezekiah picked prayer and humility instead of pride and rushing to respond. He cried out and God heard his prayers and took care of the situation quite decisively.[7] Following his deliverance from the Assyrians, Hezekiah became ill and was told by the prophet that he was going to die. Hezekiah once again humbly cried out to the Lord and God heard his prayers. Often, we are decisive and then ask God to bless it, but in Hezekiah's correct assessment of himself and his God, he knew to pray first.

Father, help us depend on You through prayer
in new ways. Hear our prayers, Lord.

Hezekiah's humble leadership was compelling to a people that had lived through cycles of broken leaders operating out of what they wanted and not the Lord—people who sacrificed divine preferences on the altar of their own preferences. In the young king's humility, he sought the Lord and obeyed. His exemplary leadership offers us clarity: Humility does not equal passivity, and lowliness doesn't mean going with the flow. This is the beautiful partnership of humility and power, perfectly personified in Jesus. No one is more compelling.

Returning to the original definition offered in chapter one, humility is the simple and freeing agreement of the biblical assessment of who God is and who I am. This humility is rooted in our belovedness and adoption of the Father so we aren't tricked into timidity or convinced to feel like a worm. This humility is walked out in friendship with Jesus, relying on His example and grace when we falter and initiated and empowered by the Holy Spirit. *This posture cannot help but be compelling to those who encounter these sorts of men and women.*

We believe we must compel people with our persona when really it's just a Person—Jesus—and all of His character developed and expressed in you and me.

A PRACTICE TO DEVELOP
COMPELLING HUMILITY

All right, y'all, we are going to get down and dirty. One of the most compelling acts of Christ's humility was when He finished dinner with His disciples, those twelve men with dusty and stinky feet, then wrapped a towel around His waist and washed their feet. I have been a part of multiple foot-washing services, or elements within a service, and it always wrecks me in a good way. I remember a time during our dating years that I asked my sweet KP if I could wash her feet (I'm no super Christian, but I got her...she's my bride!) while visiting her at her summer job. It was very significant for us...I should probably wash them again.

So, who could you serve this way? Ask the Lord and follow His lead. Could you, seriously, take the step to kneel down, wash their feet, and pray over them? Maybe you ask to serve your pastor this way, your spouse, your kids, your small group or accountability partner. Maybe it is sensitively explained and offered to a friend who does not yet know Jesus. What if this was an opportunity that offered space to share about Christ's humility and His longing to be their friend, their savior, and King. The Lord will lead you; don't do anything weird and get me in trouble, but trust the Spirit.

To get started, read John 13:1–17 and notice the end of this passage:

> *"Now that I, your Lord and Teacher, have washed your feet, you also should wash one another's feet. I have set you an example that you should do as I have done for you. Very truly I tell you, no servant is greater than his master, nor is a messenger greater than the one who sent him. Now that you know these things, you will be blessed if you do them."*

Go ahead and meditate on these words, pray for whom you could love this way, and take the courageous next step.

Lord, thank You that You captivate and compel us with Your love and humility. You are compellingly humble, whether it is washing feet or dying on the cross for our sins. We are grateful!

And Lord, if anything written in this chapter is not of You and is unhelpful for the reader's formation in Christ-likeness, help them skip pages and forget my words. If anything from this chapter would be of You, would it find fertile ground in their hearts and produce fruit, humility, and more, in their lives. Amen.

Chapter 9

Catalytic

*"If my people, who are called by my name,
will humble themselves and pray and seek my face
and turn from their wicked ways, then I will
hear from heaven, and I will forgive their sin
and will heal their land."*

2 CHRONICLES 7:14

"Do you wish to rise? Begin by descending.
You plan a tower that will pierce the clouds?
Lay first the foundation of humility."

SAINT AUGUSTINE

In chemistry, there is a simple concept that packs a punch called a catalyst. A catalyst is simply an entity—it can be a substance, event, person, etc.—that accelerates or causes a reaction or event. What "catalyzed" the Asbury Outpouring?

As I said in the first chapters of this book, there is no specific process that will 1, 2, 3, and poof…produce an outpouring. Was it a sermon? Was it the worship? What about the room, lighting, or carpet? What I saw, being weaved throughout and saturating seemingly everything, was that which we've been discussing for the entire book—humility. Radical humility drives us to radical and bold prayers for revival, convicts us to pursue unity across racial, theological, and experiential boundaries, and draws us to linger and wait in His presence. Might radical humility be the least common denominator of all of the other ingredients we are drawn to highlight and declare, "That was it! That's what we need for a move of God!"

In the early days of the Outpouring, many of us said, "Radical humility, purity, and hunger are the kindling that God has caught fire."

To this day, and until this book is tattered and forgotten, I will continue to say it. We saw it, we felt it, and we saw God move on it. Some expressions of deep humility are meaningful memories and points of learning I will carry for the rest of my life. One story must be told. It happened the day before I preached my sermon, and its core is radical humility.

On February 7, the day before my chapel service, the president of Asbury, Dr. Kevin Brown, and a local pastor, Shea Brown, held a meaningful event that they called a Witnessing

Circle. Pastor Shea Brown works in the county clerk's office and has easy access to the disheartening records of the slave trade in Lexington and the surrounding areas. Pastor Brown, a Black man, and Dr. Brown, a white man, hosted this event in which the deeds of slave owners were read aloud. Like an Old Testament Solemn Assembly,[1] this sobering act occurred during a typical week on the Asbury campus. It concluded with two of my dear friends singing the Black national anthem, "Lift Every Voice and Sing," after which the gospel choir met for practice in Hughes to prepare for chapel on the eighth. This courageous choir worshipped and prayed into the night, preparing for service the next day. These moments, this event, were saturated with sobering humility and humble leadership from leaders who are rooted at Asbury University.

I first heard this story, of the event occurring on the seventh, months after the sixteen days concluded. I wept. These brave men humbly did the hard work on the seventh that churned up the soil of humility and readiness on the eighth. Consecration, raw honesty, and humble reconciliation served as a preparatory catalyst for what was coming our way. I believe racial reconciliation is an outcome of awakening and a needed Fruit of revival, but it starts with radical humility.

More evidence of radical humility were the catalytic prayers of the contending community and many others who called for renewal and awakening in the Church, for Gen Z, and beyond. My friend Dr. Thomas has practiced, studied, and taught on travailing prayer for years. He and other friends host an event for emerging Gen Z leaders called the Awakening Project, which was held in Hughes the summer before the Outpouring and in which prayer was front and center. Prayers for renewal and awakening like I had never heard before spilled out at the altar months before February 8, 2023. Prayers throughout Wilmore, Kentucky, the United States, and around the globe have been pouring out, like incense, for decades for something like this to occur.

I have been challenged and moved by this passion and depth of prayer. But, without being a provocateur or punk, I still believe the root of this sort of prayer is humble desperation and not might or style. In Luke 18, Jesus tells the parable of the tax collector and the Pharisee. One prayed beautifully and articulately and the other prayed with radical humility begging for mercy. The latter, the tax collector's prayers, resulted in righteousness, but the impressive and epic prayers of the religious man did not. Authentic, humble prayers, desperate for God to move, are the genesis point.

Pinpointing a single event or action that ignited the Outpouring is unhelpful and unrealistic. Part of embracing the mystery of God includes giving up the need to name the cause. When something like the Asbury Outpouring happens, no one is meant to carry the burden of being the one who "started it." I thank God for that. That said, I pray this book tells those stories to stir your redemptive imagination of what God can do when His people humble themselves and go low.

Cast down your crown and see what is catalyzed with that sort of radical humility.

FOUR INGREDIENTS THAT CATALYZE MOVEMENT

When it became clear that the Spirit was stirring, people began to ask what started the Outpouring. It is quite a task to name something that cannot be easily named, much less knit together enough description for Zoom calls, podcasts, and interviews. From the first days and until now, Christ's humility was hosted by our clumsy humility. It felt like two friends reuniting and settling in together. It captivated me before the Outpouring, it captivated me and changed me during, and it continues to stir me to tears today, giving me deep hope for the future. That powerful humility was stirred by five things at Asbury:

> **Set-Apart Spaces**—Across the center of the stage, right above the organ, are the words *Holiness unto The Lord*. This is a space, through highs and lows, that has prioritized Christian holiness, rooted in the Wesleyan holiness family, for decades. Leadership has taken it on the chin when they say hard nos and made difficult calls for the sake of holiness and keeping their campus, their chapel, set apart for their purpose of training up students and leaders in the name of Jesus. Consecration is hard and costly, but exponential in Kingdom potential. Some might call it old-school or prudish, I myself have eye-rolled at institutions like Asbury at points, but what if we reclaimed the truth that it might be better spelled *b-i-b-l-i-c-a-l*.... yeah, biblical...not old-school?
>
> In a moment of catalytic movement in the Old Testament, the leader of the Israelites, Joshua, was told to say these words to his people: *"Consecrate yourselves, for tomorrow the LORD will do amazing things among you"* (Josh. 3:5)...Might we do the same. Consecration is catalytic...and consecration is a humble response to God's holiness and our desire to be prepared.

Praying Community—Isaiah 62:7 reads, "*and give him no rest till he establishes Jerusalem and makes her the praise of the earth.*" This sort of gritty, persistent, contending prayer is well known at Asbury and in Wilmore. Many staff and multiple Wilmorians know about the 1970 revival that happened in the same space, and some connect it with the global Jesus Movement. Within that cultural moment and the generational transition, they have been contending for God to move. These sorts of prayers cannot be prayed by egotistical and self-sufficient disciples but only by desperate and humbled hearts. Psalm 10:7 tells us, "*O LORD, You have heard the desire of the humble; You will strengthen their heart, You will incline Your ear*" (NASB). Like Jacob wrestling with God, Hannah prays so incoherently that the priest thought she was intoxicated, or Elijah praying in the posture of childbirth...the humble and desperate person contends.

How would radical humility and desperation impact the way you pray?

Jesus Focused—If we believe Christ is King and above everything else, why do we allow other things to sit on or share in His throne in our hearts, organizations, or even our programs and expressions? In a world and among a generation that often operates with "Christ and _____," we must demote everything else to second, third, fourth priority and set our eyes on Jesus and place Him in His rightful place in our hearts. This requires a humble self-assessment and a willingness to make courageous steps to elevate King Jesus to the correct place in our hearts.

This was continually a work at the Outpouring because we were dealing with very real humans. Humans have the innate ability to get this wrong. Often visitors wanted signs and wonders, power encounters, and charisma, and even in moments that the Spirit manifested, we continued to point to Jesus, just like the Spirit would in perfect humility. At times when the concept of "revival" was being discussed and debated, we would point back to the One who was in our midst...which was enough. A community that has humbly picked and elevated Jesus over decades became fertile soil for this catalytic encounter.

Crushed Egos—Timothy Keller tells us, "The truly gospel-humble person is a self-forgetful person whose ego is just like his or her toes. It just works. It does not draw attention to itself. The toes just work; the ego just works. Neither draws attention to itself."[2]

Ego was rightfully working as toes and to the best of the ability of those at Asbury during the Outpouring and prior fought for this sort of humility. Like we spoke about earlier in chapter four, "Crushing," we have the invite for our pride to be crushed and for our ego to operate in its rightful and God-honoring way. Is pride present on the small liberal arts college of Asbury? Definitely. Are all people in Wilmore floating on clouds, attending seminary or school and singing hymns? No. But what I saw was a real intentional dying of self and God-honoring posture of humility. A multitude of diverse denominational leaders engaged in humility with one another and some of the greatest scholars in biblical literature and theology unloaded snacks, held doors, and followed the leadership of nineteen- to twenty-one-year-olds.

There is something about the weight of God's glory that just orients our egos beautifully.

Not only was humility permeating through communication and the ministry, Christ's crushed, crucified, and then risen and glorified self was being encountered and worshipped. Like a perfect cocktail of crushing and lowliness, Christ's and our feeble efforts, this sort of worship was poured out at His feet.

Courageous Yeses—The multitude of yeses that led to what God was doing required radical humility. Is that not the reality all throughout Scripture and history? A call from God, encounter with God, an evil or injustice revealed, and a humble "yes" from a man or woman to step up. Abraham had a humble and courageous "yes" to go to a land he had yet to know. Moses, confronted at the burning bush, humbly went out with many questions and leaned on his brother Aaron to free the Israelites. Fast-forward to Mary, a humble "yes" when the angel came along with her fiancé with humility to stay and listen to the angel to parent the coming baby boy. A humble person's "yes" colliding with a catalyst from God can do much for the Kingdom. We saw this first-hand with police officers, pastors, baristas, professors, and musical artists. Humble and courageous "yeses" curating and stewarding a fresh Outpouring of God.

I DON'T WANT TO RUN OUT

In 2 Kings 4, we are introduced to a widow who needed a move of God. This widow was married to a godly man who had been in community with and served alongside God's prophet Elisha but he had since passed. This left the woman alone with two sons who were going to be taken into slavery, lawfully though heartbreaking, by a debtor. This mom was a good and godly woman who was afraid of losing her next generation. Does this sound familiar? Might we relate? Concerned about losing the next generation to slavery, slavery of whatever you want to name, and feeling pretty hopeless and needing help. She cried out to the prophet Elisha and he responded, "What do you have in the house?" This would be a humbling question, and without hope, possibly humiliating. Elisha is told about a jar of oil that she has, possibly for anointing or for cooking, and he tells her, "*Go, borrow vessels from everywhere, from all your neighbors— empty vessels; do not gather just a few. And when you have come in, you shall shut the door behind you and your sons; then pour it into all those vessels, and set aside the full ones*" (NKJV).

Can you imagine what happened next? The mother and sons dispersed and started knocking on doors, asking for empty vessels. My friend Ed painted this picture beautifully, placing it perfectly in my southern American context. Sons and a mom knocking on doors asking for empty flour pots and emptied out vegetable oil bottles. The famous, or infamous, "Oh bless your heart" rushing out of their neighbors' mouths. "Honey, it's been a hard season for you losing your dad…you can have the flour and oil too!"

"Well, thank you, ma'am…it has been hard…we are up against these debtors…I know this sounds weird but actually empty out the flour, oil, the eggs from your egg cartons…I just need empty vessels."

Don't we do this often? God wants us empty but we don't understand. We want to offer a lot more but He asks for empty. A vessel full of oil, wine, flour, or whatever was not helpful in this moment…it needed to be empty. Often, I might come 30 percent full…maybe 85 percent…who knows. The reality is that that leaves 30 percent of the vessel unable to be filled by the miracle. Like 25 percent of my mug full of cold and old coffee, I would only benefit from 75 percent of fresh joe. If God's miracle is coming, I want 100 percent, not just 75 percent. This requires trusting humility…not taking handouts from all our neighbors. Taking empty vessels. Not bringing impressive offerings, but empty and humbled ones.

Question for you: Did these vessels need to be large and strong? Beautiful and consecrated for the purposes of a miracle? How big? A specific color?

No…empty.

There were no other specifications besides empty. How might this free you as you long for a catalytic move of God or really, honestly, just an encounter in your blue chair, prayer room, or the pulpit at your local church? Muster up, fill it to the brim, and wait? Or empty yourselves, with a vessel of integrity and strength (that has gone through the crucible) but with nothing else inside besides humility and surrendered potential for a fresh outpouring and filling? Eastern religions focus on meditations and practices to empty for the sake of emptiness and peace. We empty ourselves to be filled, filled by the Spirit of God.

So the empty vessels are brought inside by the sons and the widow starts pouring the little bit of oil she has left. "She poured it out"…no hesitation or saving some just in case… poured it out. In moments like these, can we relate? Feeling pretty spent, do we think that if God doesn't come through, we might need to hold on to some? I get it, there's wisdom there, but when God's prophet tells her to pour it out and fill these vessels, she was not hesitating. Imagine a little vessel of oil, possibly something like a mason jar, being poured out into these big vessels and it just kept flowing and flowing. It kept pouring and filling until she said to her sons, "Bring me another vessel," and her sons respond, "There is not another vessel." When God is miraculously moving, outpouring His oil, I don't want to run out of empty vessels. If the oil of God is endlessly being multiplied from a little to filling vessels, let's not wish we spent a bit more time gathering empty vessels… "Bummer, I wish we'd emptied more!" Minister Alexander MacLaren said,

"You have God in the measure in which you desire Him. Only remember that the desire that brings God must be more than a feeble, fleeting wish. Wishing is one thing; *willing* is quite another. Lazily wishing and strenuously desiring are two entirely different postures of mind; the former gets nothing and the latter gets everything, gets God, and with God all that God can bring."[3]

Are we willing to gather empty vessels? Soberly we must remember, when the empty vessels stopped, the oil stopped.

Empty vessels are not stagnant or sitting on a shelf in this story, they are catalytic opportunities for a supernatural filling for the sake of others, in this case the next generation. Empty is quite a humble state, isn't it? I write this and head toward the end of this book and desire it to be helpful and engaging, enjoyable and authentic, but it is just an empty vessel. These words, learnings, and stories are just the bottom and walls of a vessel that the Spirit of God must saturate and fill for you to get really much out of it. Our preaching is the same, a vessel for God's filling. Our degrees, any and all you want to get, or careers are the same. Sturdy and wonderful vessels but as Christians, we cannot be filled by them. I see the gathering of empty vessels like the gathering of resources the Old Testament leaders would get together to make an altar to God. Our empty vessels are altars for God to move upon. Or for my young parents, like our kid's coil pots, little clay pots that are built up, one by one, by little "snakes" rolled out from clay. One row built upon another row, and upon another, and so on. Our achievements, our expertise, or competencies, and all the other beautiful things you bring just strengthen the vessel and possibly even expand the capacity for more. But it does not fill us, God does. And when He is miraculously pouring out, I just don't want to run out or compete with what He has for me with other things filling me up.

What do I mean by empty? How do we empty ourselves in humility and preparation? Here are some tools that have helped me...

- **Confession**—Emptying ourselves of our sins and ick and handing them to Jesus in humility and with contrite hearts. Doing this regularly with safe friends is a gift from the Church to you.

- **Posture**—How do you see what you have and have achieved? Filling you up or just strengthening and expanding the vessel? Has the hard work you've done filled your vessel or just tested it and tried it, strengthening its resilience and ability to carry a fresh filling?
- **Worship**—When we worship, we pour out ourselves at the feet of Jesus, leaving us fully aware of who we are and who He is. Worship empties ourselves of ourselves and fills us back up with hope... a fresh filling of the Spirit.
- **Perspective**—Celebrate ways you've partnered with God to strengthen and expand capacity, either with achievements and milestones you've achieved or circumstances and difficulty that have tested and strengthened you. Remember, tempering is hard but good... it's the humble work of preparation.

Also, remember we have some good models for empty, don't we? The spine to our conversation on humility is a passage we've mentioned often, Philippians 2. The emptying, or kenotic, passage explaining the work Christ did for our sake. He emptied Himself and took on the form of a human, Creator putting on creature, to serve us. He served us to the point of death, a criminal's death on the cross. He was humiliated so we don't have to be.

He was humiliated so that we, in Him, can just experience humility.

This emptied-out savior was placed in a humble and empty home, Mary's womb. Out of all the places where Christ could arrive, it was a humble and empty vessel. A teenager engaged to a humble carpenter, with an empty womb, would be the precious home for baby Jesus in His most vulnerable state. The birth, into an empty manger, humble and confrontationally countercultural to where anyone would think of birthing royalty. When Christ grew and set out in His public ministry, He encountered many men and women who were empty-handed; hungry folks gathered to listen to Him teach, empty-handed and hopeless after years of paralyzation, blindness, or bleeding, empty-handed and discouraged disciples terrified and disappointed after Christ had died, and the glory of the empty tomb. Empty is brimming with potential, just like humility.

So, if 327 folks read this book, my prayer is that we have 327 more empty vessels that are entrustable and prepared for a fresh outpouring of His Spirit. If more, praise God because we could use more empty vessels. Imagine the potential of more empty, humble, and entrustable vessels for fresh outpourings of God like we experienced at Asbury for those short sixteen days. Might outpouring stir up renewal, renewal across a country and globe reviving the Church, and that sustained leads to an awakening. And possibly, just hoping, this sort of movement might hasten the day of Christ's return. Could empty and humble vessels willing to empty themselves and open to be sent and placed around the world, maybe in the most unreached places on the globe, to be a part of completing the Great Commission? This sort of thing is catalytic. Pursing humility, picking it, and doing the work it requires could be the very thing we need!

THE CATALYST

A catalyst is a substance that is introduced to another substance or substances that evokes or increases a reaction. This word could be applied to many things, like a game-changing play in a sport, a controversial piece of art sparking a debate, or a heart-moving speech that evokes compassion and response. A humility that is deeply formed by spiritual practices, spurred on and shaped by the Spirit and rooted in Christ, can be the most catalytic characteristic and posture in the world. This sturdy lowliness enters in, really rooted and unchanging, and increases and evokes change. Within faith, yes, but in many other realms of culture; powerfully corrective and offensive in politics, countercultural and refreshing in business, stirring up vibrancy and usefulness in education and research, along with restorative and healing in relationships, families, and marriage. I am not trying to be an infomercial on this magic drug that will help you lose weight, get ripped, and have better hair, but I hope this underengaged and undervalued deeply Christian value has a resurgence. When the world tells us that we have to get stronger, do more, and fight for our seat at the table and hold our space in culture...let us not forget humility...let us not forsake what seeped out of every pore and saturated every interaction of the Man we adore and worship, Jesus. Many times, we place humility on the shelf to fight for Christianity and its place and convictions...why would we sacrifice one of the two words Christ gave to Himself, to His very heart, to promote and proclaim Jesus.

Humility is a catalyst for cultural change...and Christ is its perfect example and purest source.

Please, don't forsake humility "for the sake of Jesus" because (1) it doesn't make sense, (2) whatever you're interacting with needs Jesus and not you, and (3) you misrepresent humble Jesus.

Now, the danger of writing a book on humility and the formation, expression, and potential of it is that it sneakily, outside of my will, slips into another self-help book with verses and quotes throughout. Another concern is that it slips into religion...longing and striving for humility without breathing deep and allowing Christ to form to express Himself in us. The beauty of this is that Christ is aware and equally concerned with who we are, who we are becoming, and what we do. Christ is intentionally, via the Spirit, working within those three things and directing and forming us. These are not silos and compartments of our lives but intertwined and woven together in our journey of apprenticing with Jesus. The fact we must remember in all of this is that Christ is humble, Humble with a capital *H*, and He is our goal and the target of all of our affection, not a character trait. We are not pursuing humility nearly as intensely as Humble is pursuing us. Jesus is chasing us down, forming us, and transforming us, and we can rest in this.

Because of this truth, we must remember that we are not the catalyst nor is our humility, really. It is Christ moving on, pouring out over our humble and submitted hearts. Christ is the catalyst. Like science, His incarnation introduced an unchanging Jesus that has evoked and increased rapid change. His humility introduced into the world catalyzed a movement that is occurring thousands of years later. Hopefully Christ and the cross have catalyzed this same thing in your life as well! Yes, Scripture calls us to humble ourselves, which we've explored and read over and over again in these pages, but that is just preparing for Christ to move. Humility is like dry firewood, practices to deepen and enrich humility are like lighter fluid, and Christ's power and encounter are the spark. The fire, Jesus, will lead us in humility until eternity in heaven.

A CATALYTIC PRACTICE FOR
OUR HUMILITY

One of the first Bible studies I ever went to was one led by a friend's father, Doug, who was a part of a ministry that loved God's Word unlike many I have encountered. I remember early on, before I had accepted Jesus and even soon after, being so intimidated by their passion for memorizing Scripture. Over time, I was convinced of the power of memorized Scripture and hiding God's words in our hearts. That's the next, and last, suggested practice. As we pursue humility and rest in the catalytic potential of it, and in Christ's catalytic humility in the story we find ourselves in, let's memorize Philippians 2:1–11. I have memorized it in the Amplified version because I enjoy the added explanations...you can choose whatever version you would like.

In hungry humility, not religious obligation or striving, hide these words in your heart and pray with me that it would produce fruit in our lives. Philippians 2:3–7 (AMP) says,

> *Do nothing from selfishness or empty conceit [through factional motives, or strife], but with [an attitude of] humility [being neither arrogant nor self-righteous], regard others as more important than yourselves. Do not merely look out for your own personal interests, but also for the interests of others. Have this same attitude in*

yourselves which was in Christ Jesus [look to Him as your example in selfless humility], who, although He existed in the form and unchanging essence of God [as One with Him, possessing the fullness of all the divine attributes— the entire nature of deity], did not regard equality with God a thing to be grasped or asserted [as if He did not already possess it, or was afraid of losing it]; but emptied Himself [without renouncing or diminishing His deity, but only temporarily giving up the outward expression of divine equality and His rightful dignity] by assuming the form of a bond-servant, and being made in the likeness of men [He became completely human but was without sin, being fully God and fully man].

Lord, if any of this is not of You and not any help for the reader's formation, equipping, and encouragement, help them forget it, but if there was anything from Your Spirit that would benefit their journey and Your mission, will it land in fertile and churned-up soil in their souls. Amen.

Conclusion

The Culmination

On Friday, February 24, I was given the privilege of speaking to the Asbury student body at their chapel service directly following those sixteen powerful days. Some students and staff were exhausted, some were angry, some were ready to go for another couple of months. The emotions and opinions in the chapel, across campus, and around the world were numerous, diverse, and weighty. There was a sobriety, a great sense of gratitude, and a real humility on that day on campus and in that chapel service.

It was a deep breath mixed with a deep sadness.

My dear friend Kevin had worked faithfully with his staff at Asbury through the Outpouring to check on morale and capacity while also hosting tens of thousands of surprise guests. It was heroic and those finals days at Asbury were an absolute clinic on maneuvering through expectations and accusations, practical needs and ethereal questions, and our own strong opinions and exhaustion. After a couple days of discernment, we did not make the decision to close down but instead to catalyze. Instead of closing the lid, it was time to burst and saturate spaces with the testimony and hope that the Asbury Outpouring gave us.

We had collectively and individually been confronted by God's presence, led through the crucible, and in many ways had our "crushing seasons" dignified as the "new wine" was served. In the culmination of the Asbury Outpouring we could rest in the fact that we, and the very institutions represented, were creatures with limits and God did not expect a university to become an event venue/resort or the team to become the Avengers. We did our best walking in consecrated confidence during those days and within those decisions with Christ-like character only produced and kept by the Holy Spirit bearing fruit in us. The humility, kindness, and gentleness experienced at Asbury had compelled many and now we would see if it would serve as a catalyst. I believe it has and still is.

WHO IS WORTHY?

As I think of a person and place saturated with humility and absolutely humble, far be it from me to think of anyone but Jesus or anyplace but heaven. The reality is that I had not really thought about heaven at all in my early journey with Jesus. I did not come to Jesus because I was afraid of hell and wanted a ticket to heaven. But over the last couple years, spurred on by our journey with Esther, I think about heaven often. No more sadness or sickness. No more bullies nor pride. No more tears and no more division. Restored and perfectly humble. It's a place that only one person wears a crown and all of creation is doing what it's made to do, worshipping and bowing to the King of Kings. Heaven and humility...I have tears running down my chubby cheeks when I think of how beautiful it will be.

Conclusion

The culmination of all things in heaven is the great crowning of Jesus in all of His glory and honor and invites all of creation into their rightful place, humility.

In the last book of the Bible, we get to read about the second coming of Jesus through the prophetic vision of the apostle John. This book of the Bible is a sneak peak of the "grand finale" of all things. We read about Christ's return but are also invited to see a place, heaven. This is where everything is set right. Just capital *H* Humility, my nickname for Jesus, receiving what is due to Him.

Humility was never just a concept or characteristic; it has always been a Person.

In the fourth chapter of Revelation, we get a peek into the Throne Room of heaven. The door was open and John was invited to see. There was a throne...imagine it now...with one who looked like jasper and ruby with a rainbow circling this throne. Around this throne were twenty-four people in dazzling white with crowns upon their heads. There were flashes of lightning and booms of thunder. How could you have pride in His presence? No one in the Throne Room could. Pride became utterly impossible—as impossible as sadness or sin. In the vision, there were these four "living creatures" that would sing night and day of His holiness as the twenty-four people surrounding the throne would fall down and lay their crowns down at His feet.

Crowns, in the presence of God in the Throne Room, should be handled like "hot potato"...get them off your head and out of your hands as fast as you can! No one will wear a crown in the Throne Room besides Jesus...this is heavenly humility.

"Who is worthy to open the scroll and look inside?" an angel asked. John realized quickly that no one was worthy...

absolutely humbled. Then an elder redirected John's downtrodden face with a declaration. "Do not weep. See, the lion of the tribe of Judah, the root of David, has triumphed. He is able to open the scroll and the seven seals." John raised his chin and saw a slain Lamb, Jesus, standing at the center of the throne huddled by the four living creatures and elders. As soon as the Lamb took the scroll, the four creatures and elders fell on their faces with a harp in one hand and golden bowls containing the beautifully fragrant prayers of God's people in the other. "Worthy" they sang...and then thousands upon thousands of angels began to sing out as well of His worthiness. There was no pride, no ego, no looking to the right and to the left seeing how one sized up compared to the other. All eyes were on Jesus and there was a collective focus on praising the Humble King, the Lamb who was slain.

Heavenly humility exudes again when John looks and there is an uncountable group of people. They were not all white. They were not all Black. They spoke and sung in different languages. Some were tall and some were small. None of this mattered like it does on earth because of our pride, sin, and brokenness. Heavenly humility, a unified gaze, and praise focused on Jesus brought every tribe, tongue, and nation together to declare "Salvation belong to our God, who sit on the throne, and to the Lamb!" These multitudes just join in with the angels, elders, and creatures in unending worship.

The picture that Jesus paints through the apostle John's epistle, the last book of the Bible, is like looking over the edge of the Grand Canyon or standing at the base of the largest redwood tree...awe-inspiring and humbling. Things like this force our self-awareness and right assessment...we are small and those are big. Just like this, we read of John's first encounter in the throne room with the Lamb and cannot help but be humbled. Being in these places and reading these passages are good for our souls. Like the elders and four creatures casting their crowns and falling on their face, seeing Jesus in all of His glory has no other optional response. It will always be humility. And in his midst, in all of His glory in heaven, there will be no pride, no competition, no comparison or insecurity. Just worship.

All of heaven is humble. Golden streets, a gorgeous throne, our Humble King, and our only capable response, humble worship.

CHOCOLATE MILK TOASTS

One of my favorite things to do is to take my daughters to local coffee shops for a chocolate milk date. My Eden and I try to do this weekly and we are now unpacking sweet things like friends at school, questions about faith, and like every seven-year-old, telling potty jokes. Mercy, who is 1.5 as I write this, can get down on some chocolate milk but often wants my cappuccino foam as well. These are cherished times that I will remember forever and ever and I hope they do as well. The Lord spoke to me through chocolate milk dates a few years ago and humbled me with a heavenly perspective. I never really thought about heaven nor studied or preached about it. Now I think about it all the time. Why? Because heaven will have unbelievable chocolate milk to share with my daughter Esther.

Most Fridays, I snag a cappuccino and a chocolate milk and drive across town to Esther's grave, which we call "her garden" for Eden's sake. These mornings sound morbid, and maybe they are, but they are my weekly reminders of our humanity, finality, and the fact that Esther is enjoying glory...maybe a bit like those images we read about in Revelation. The fall, along with Satan, and the brokenness and sickness it created in the world stole my chocolate milk dates with Esther, so we do this. We also did a chocolate milk toast at her celebration of life. These chocolate milk dates remind me of something very humbling. During one of my chocolate milk dates at Esther's garden, I sat under a tree and processed via poetry...

The Beauty of Expiration Dates

Expiration dates brought me curdled milk, green fuzz, and strange stinks. Expiration dates brought me to the DMV for renewals, phone calls with companies, and more administration.

Food gets stinky and stale, licenses must be renewed, and coupons can't be used anymore. This mysterious date stated by someone establishes finality that I must respond to. I honestly hate them.

Or I hated them.

As I drive through beautiful stone pillars with a steel gate swung open, I whisper... "there's an expiration date." As I drive by memorials, mausoleums, and memories...I trust there is an expiration date. I arrive at the "garden of innocence," declaring this wasn't your design and that there is an expiration date.

This expiration date doesn't come with stink, stress, or sting. This expiration date is not proclaimed by a date printed on a label or license. This expiration date doesn't get highlighted by a strange mold on bread or discolored sour cream. This expiration date comes to us on clouds and a mighty sound of a trumpet.

There's an expiration date on cemeteries, heartbreak, doctor appointments, and graves for children. There is an expiration date on pride, sickness, and grief. Hunger, hatred, and homelessness will expire as the King comes back, bright like fire, and pulls us out of the muck and the mire. As He comes on the clouds with that mighty white horse, we of course will fall to our knees and proclaim Him as Lord and thank Him for this holy expiration date.

So, would you let mold, stink, and DMV trips remind you of this holy expiration date? The rocks and trees will cry out... what about mold in your fridge? There is a beautiful expiration date we believe in, work towards, and wait for. I long for that day... and mold and stink have a way to say remember today that come what may, He has provided a heavenly getaway.

The reality is that there is an expiration date on all of this. On pride, striving, insecurity. On success, shininess, and champions. When we get to heaven and experience the great culmination, there will be the ceasing of both suffering and success. There will be humility. Every knee will bow, and tongue confess that there is only one God and we are not rulers nor the god of our own lives. Every knee will bend in realization that our striving, achievements, and luxury condos don't mean much in these moments. We will confess that Jesus is Lord. Radical humility, heavenly humility, utter humility. That will be a good day...and I'll hopefully (though I don't really want to argue this theologically) enjoy a chocolate milk date with Esther for the first time while we worship the only One who deserves it, Jesus. All of us, in heaven, worshiping capital *H* Humble, humbled and grateful we get to set eyes on the King of glory and do not have to carry the weight of those clunky crowns that we were never designed to carry but just dump at His feet.

Heaven is humble and we will enjoy it greatly. Until then, your Humble King is here to journey with you Lower.

As you journey, have a chocolate milk toast for humility.

Cheers to going lower.

Acknowledgments

I have many reasons to be the most grateful man you've ever met. Besides my greatest gratitude for being beloved by the Father, rescued by Jesus, and empowered by the Spirit, I am also immensely grateful for . . .

Kristin—Thank you, sweet KP, for being safe, my champion, and for walking me from pride into a little less pride. Your consecrated confidence and comfort in the hidden places of life, vocation, and our family are challenging to me and greatly impactful. I love you!

Eden—Thanks for letting me hide at my desk and crank this book out, sweet one. Thank you for leading alongside me, teaching me, and believing in me. I see you and your tremendous gifting, and I pray whatever I get to be a part of is eclipsed by the adventures, impact, and intimacy with Jesus that you experience in your life.

Esther—Oh how I miss you. I can't imagine being at this place without my time on earth parenting you and now the good and bad days remembering you and missing you. Possibly no one on earth has taught me more than you, sweet girl. Enjoy some heavenly chocolate milk.

Acknowledgments

Mercy—You make my soul belly laugh and my hope rise. I love you so much and am grateful that you'd come sit on my lap and give me random hugs and waves as I wrote. I pray that anything I have been a part of and in any way God has used me would be multiplied tenfold in your life, my sweet Mercy.

Mama Miriam—I am grateful for you, Mom, and your consistent curiosity on what I'm learning, how I am experiencing my faith, and cheering on this book. Thank you for introducing me to a love for reading and always having books all over the house.

Asbury University staff & students—Asbury, thank you. I'm grateful for how you've received me as one of your own, stewarded the Outpouring with humility and sobriety, and have lived out the active wrestling and application of what we all learned. Kevin, Sarah, Greg, Jeannie, Rob, and many more… you are heroes, sacrificial hosts, servant-hearted practitioners, and tremendous teammates.

Brian Scott—You've taught many, myself included, about a new way to lead. I am grateful for how you drove me into Philippians 2 and challenged me to live and lead from that posture…the posture of radical humility. I am thankful for how you exemplify this posture and challenge many to lead and serve from a place of humility.

Andrew, Justin, and Curt—Brothers, I am grateful for your steady and courageous friendship. You all have both faithfully suffered and celebrated with me. Thank you for journeying so closely in the last years of my walk with Jesus. You know all my junk, believe in me still, and fight for my soul.

Ken Baldes—To one of the most humble and hidden leaders I've ever known. Thank you for teaching me about priorities,

Acknowledgments

prayer, and a love that introduced me to Jesus over and over again.

David Thomas & the NewRoom family—Thank you for gritty and faithful contending prayer and hard work sowing for what we are living in now. David, thanks for your commitment to me in the good along with the ugly and messy.

Samwise Thorner—Thank you for exemplifying consecrated confidence. I am grateful for how you've walked alongside me in very high highs and many low lows all with the same heart and message... that I am loved.

New City Church—Thanks for teaching me so much about humility and leading for the sake of others and not a platform. I miss you!

My little brothers in the faith—Thanks to the mighty men who have invited me into their lives to cheer on, encourage, and equip to walk as humbly with the Lord as we can... together. I love you and believe in you... you know who you are.

Thomas Dean—To my big brother, who has walked me through this process... somehow, we've done it, Tom! I'm grateful for how you've advocated for me, cheered me on, and laughed with me about how wild this season is.

Jenny Baumgartner—Thank you for your perseverance and faithfulness as the editor of this story, my first book, while stewarding all sorts of dynamics and circumstances... faithful and kind to me and what's been my heart. I'm grateful for you and your team!

Mama Dori & Papa Jeff—I simply could not imagine this season without your sacrificial love and support of the girls and me. We simply could not have done it. Your prayers and encouragement mean so much. Thanks for raising such a strong and steady teammate for me...KP and I love you both!

You, the reader—Thank you for picking up a book on humility and hungering for a move of God wherever you find yourself. Lean in...pick humility...and wait upon the Lord. He is on the move!

Notes

Introduction: An Ordinary & Unremarkable Chapel Service
1. Robert M. Mulholland Jr. and Ruth Haley Barton, *Invitation to a Journey: A Road Map for Spiritual Formation* (Lisle, IL: InterVarsity Press, 2016), 19.

Chapter 1: Going Lower
1. Romans 8:14–17
2. John 15:15
3. John 14:16,16:7–15
4. C. S. Lewis, *Mere Christianity* (Mercy House, 2020).

Chapter 2: Confrontation
1. Genesis 12:1–3
2. Genesis 22:1–18
3. Genesis 32:26
4. Genesis 32:28
5. Robert M. Mulholland Jr. and Ruth Haley Barton, *Invitation to a Journey: A Road Map for Spiritual Formation* (Lisle, IL: InterVarsity Press, 2016), 45.
6. Matthew Poole, *Matthew Poole's Commentary on the Holy Bible—Book of Philippians* (GraceWorks Multimedia, 2011).

Chapter 3: Crucible
1. Tod Bolsinger, *Tempered Resilience: How Leaders Are Formed in the Crucible of Change* (Lisle, IL: IVP, an imprint of InterVarsity Press, 2020), 114.

Chapter 4: Crushing
1. Strahan Coleman, @commonerscommunion.
2. Mark Vroegap, *Dark Clouds, Deep Mercy* (Wheaton, IL: Crossway, 2019).
3. Ibid.

Chapter 5: Creature
1. Luke 4:1–13
2. Max Lucado, "It Began in a Manger," *The Gift for All People: Thoughts on God's Great Grace* (Walker Large Print, 2003).

Notes

Chapter 7: Character

1. Luke 24:13–35
2. C. S. Lewis, *The Screwtape Letters* (San Francisco: HarperOne, 2001), 69.
3. Dane Ortlund, *Gentle and Lowly: The Heart of Christ for Sinners and Sufferers* (Wheaton, IL: Crossway Books, 2021).

Chapter 8: Compelling

1. Andrew Murray, *Humility* (Bethany House, 2001).
2. Timothy Kelly, *Walking with God Through Pain and Suffering* (New York: Penguin Books, 2016),123.
3. Rich Villodas [@richvillodas], X, February 9, 2020.
4. C. S. Lewis, *Mere Christianity*, C. S. Lewis Signature Classics (New York: HarperCollins Publishers, 2001), 128.
5. Numbers 21:4–9
6. Numbers 21:8
7. 2 Kings 19:35

Chapter 9: Catalytic

1. Joel 1:14
2. Timothy Keller, *The Freedom of Self-Forgetfulness: The Path to True Christian Joy* (La Grange, KY: 10Publishing, 2022).
3. Alexander MacLaren, *Expositions of Holy Scripture* (Baker Book House, 33 vols., 1904).

Zach Meerkreebs is the proud husband of Kristin and father to three little girls: Eden, Esther, and Mercy. He is thankful for the opportunity to have served within churches, by coaching and catalyzing church plants, traveling and speaking, and most recently had the gift of a lifetime as he preached on February 8, 2023, at Asbury University and had a front-row seat to see God moving amidst the Asbury Outpouring in a small town and experienced sixteen days of unending prayer and worship. Tens of thousands of guests from around the world experienced the peace and power of God.